Preface

Not being very good at praying, I ha
better Christians than me, drawing
These prayers reflect my personal p
traditional language as well as my a
beauty of the language, the comprehensive in scope, and theological
clarity, are very helpful, and have done much to help me communicate
daily with God.

All of the sources used for this material is online and free (see
Acknowledgments) but in creating this my idea was to put everything in
one place, in a little book I could take with me everywhere, rather than
having several books on Kindle plus a prayerbook and various printouts,
as had hitherto been the case.

The prayers come from the Lutheran, Anglican, and Presbyterian
traditions, and come in three categories:

- Individual prayers for personal faith and help, including
  'church prayers' to prepare for Sunday worship.
- Structured services from the Book of Common Prayer, adapted
  for individual devotions (eg by removing responses). Compline
  was not originally a Reformation-era service, but I have added
  some of its prayers.
- Weekly and daily prayer patterns, mostly from German sources
  (the Calvin and BCP prayers were not initially arranged on a
  week pattern – this is for structural purposes). The prayers
  from Habermann's *Christian's Companion* are accompanied by
  Lutheran hymns, which were added to the early 20th century
  translation available on Gutenberg, and I have added Scottish
  metrical psalms to the Calvin prayers.
- Additional Scottish Metrical Psalms are supplied at the end.

I hope that you find it useful. *Soli Deo Gloria!*

Angus Ker, Edinburgh, July 2020

**This publication is for personal devotional use and is not made,
nor should it be distributed, not financial profit.**

Contents

Prayers of Martin Luther

Morning: I thank Thee, my Heavenly Father, through Jesus Christ, Thy dear Son, that Thou hast kept me this night from all harm and danger; and I pray Thee to keep me this day also from sin and all evil, that all my doings and life may please Thee. For into Thy hands I commend myself, my body and soul, and all things. Let Thy holy angel be with me, that the Wicked Foe may have no power over me. Amen.

Evening: I thank Thee, my Heavenly Father, through Jesus Christ, Thy dear Son, that Thou hast graciously kept me this day, and I pray Thee to forgive me all my sins, where I have done wrong, and graciously keep me this night. For into Thy hands I commend myself, my body and soul, and all things. Let Thy holy angel be with me, that the Wicked Foe may have no power over me. Amen.

A Prayer for Assurance of Being Heard: Lord God, heavenly Father, I ask and would be assured that my petitions shall and must be nothing less than yea and amen. Otherwise I will not pray nor have intercession made for me. Not that I am righteous or worthy, for I know very well and confess that I am unworthy. I have earned Thine eternal wrath and hell fire with my great and many sins. But in this that Thou dost command and constrain me to pray in the Name of Thy dear Son, our Lord Jesus Christ, I am still somewhat obedient. Upon this challenge and consolation of Thine infinite goodness, not on account of my own righteousness, do I kneel or stand before Thee, and pray what is upon my heart concerning those who are in need of Thy help. If Thou dost not help us, O Lord, Thou wilt offend and dishonor Thy Name. Thou wilt surely spare Thyself, lest the world would say Thou wert an ungracious and dreadful God. Preserve us from such a misfortune. Remember, dear heavenly Father, how Thou hast at all times supported and helped Thy people. I will not cease to knock but will continue to cry aloud and to plead to the end of my life. Amen.

A Prayer for Love toward Others: Dear Father in heaven, for the sake of your dear Son Jesus Christ grant us your Holy Spirit, that we may be true learners of Christ, and therefore acquire a heart with a never-ceasing fountain of love. Amen

A Prayer for Lasting Peace: Dear God, give us peaceful hearts and a right courage in the confusion and strife against the devil. And so may we not only endure and finally triumph, but also have peace in the midst of the struggle. May we praise and thank you and not complain or become impatient against your divine will. Let peace win the victory in our hearts, that we may never through impatience initiate anything against you, our God, or our neighbours. May we remain quiet and peaceable toward God and toward other people, both inwardly and outwardly, until the final and eternal peace shall come. Amen.

A Prayer for Relief from Misery: Lord, misery and misfortune annoy me and oppress me. I long to be rid of them. You have said, Ask and it will be given you. So I come and ask. Amen.

Casting all your care upon Him: Heavenly Father! Thou art indeed my Lord and God, who hast made me out of nothing and redeemed me through Thy Son. Thou hast commanded and appointed me to perform these my duties and Labours, which I, however, cannot accomplish as I desire, and many troubles there be that frighten and oppress me, so that I am, as to my own power, without help and consolation; therefore I commend all things into Thy hands, do Thou help and console me, and be Thou all in all. Amen.

Prayer Before the Sermon: Eternal God and Father of our Lord Jesus Christ, give us your Holy Spirit who writes the preached Word into our hearts. May we receive and believe it and be cheered and comforted by it in eternity. Glorify your Word in our hearts and make it so bright and warm that we may find pleasure in it, through your Holy Spirit think what is right, and by your power fulfill the Word, for the sake of Jesus Christ, your Son, our Lord. Amen.

Prayer After the Sermon: Dear Lord Christ, you have enlightened my heart with your truth. Grant me your Spirit and the power to do and not to do whatever pleases your gracious will. Amen.

A Prayer for Strengthened Faith: Almighty God, through the death of your Son you have destroyed sin and death. Through his resurrection you have restored innocence and eternal life. We who are delivered from the power of the devil may live in your kingdom. Give us grace that we may believe this with our whole heart. Enable us, always, to steadfastly praise and thank you in this faith, through your Son Jesus Christ, our Lord. Amen.

A Prayer After Communion: We thank you, almighty Lord God, that you have refreshed us with this precious gift, and we ask for your mercy that you would let it nurture in us strong faith toward you and intensive love among us all, through Jesus Christ, your Son our Lord. Amen.

Prayers of John Calvin

Prayer before the Day: My God—my Father and Preserver—who of your goodness has watched over me during the past night, and brought me to this day, grant also that I may spend it wholly in the worship and service of your most holy deity. Let me not think, or say, or do a single thing which tends not to your service and submission to your will, that thus all my actions may aim at your glory and the salvation of my brethren, while they are taught by my example to serve you.
And as you are giving light to this world for the purposes of external life by the rays of the sun, so enlighten my mind by the effulgence of your Spirit, that he may guide me in the way of your righteousness.

To whatever purpose I apply my mind, may the end which I ever propose to myself be your honor and service. May I expect all happiness from your grace and goodness only. Let me not attempt anything whatever that is not pleasing to you. Grant also, that while I Labour for the maintenance of this life, and care for the things which pertain to food and raiment, I may raise my mind above them to the blessed and heavenly life which you have promised to your children.

Be pleased also, in manifesting yourself to me as the protector of my soul as well as my body, to strengthen and fortify me against all the assaults of the devil, and deliver me from all the dangers which continually beset us in this life. But seeing it is a small thing to have begun, unless I also persevere, I therefore entreat of you, O Lord, not only to be my guide and director for this day, but to keep me under your protection to the very end of life, that thus my whole course may be performed under your superintendence.

As I ought to make progress, do you add daily more and more to the gifts of your grace until I wholly adhere to your Son Jesus Christ, whom I justly regard as the true Sun, shining constantly in our minds. In order to my obtaining of you these great and manifold blessings, forget, and out of your infinite mercy, forgive my offenses, as you have promised that you will do to those who call upon you in sincerity.

Grant that I may hear your voice in the morning since I have hoped in you. Show me the way in which I should walk, since I have lifted up my soul unto you. Deliver me from my enemies, O Lord, I have fled unto you. Teach me to do your will, for you are my God.

Let your good Spirit conduct me to the land of uprightness. Amen.

Prayer before Bed: O Lord God—who has given man the night for rest, as you have created the day in which he may employ himself in Labour— grant, I pray, that my body may so rest during this night that my mind cease not to be awake to you, nor my heart faint or be overcome with torpor, preventing it from adhering steadfastly to the love of you. While laying aside my cares to relax and relieve my mind, may I not, in the meanwhile, forget you, nor may the remembrance of your goodness and grace, which ought always to be deeply engraven on my mind, escape my memory.

In like manner, also, as the body rests may my conscience enjoy rest. Grant, moreover, that in taking sleep I may not give indulgence to the flesh, but only allow myself as much as the weakness of this natural state requires, to my being enabled thereafter to be more alert in your service. Be pleased to keep me so chaste and unpolluted, not less in mind than in body, and safe from all dangers, that my sleep itself may turn to the glory of your name.

But since this day has not passed away without my having in many ways offended you through my proneness to evil, in like manner as all things are now covered by the darkness of the night, so let everything that is sinful in me lie buried in your mercy.

Hear me, O God, Father and Preserver, through Jesus Christ your Son. Amen.

Calvin Prayers & Metrical Psalms for a Week

Sunday: Grant, Almighty God, that as thou hast given us thy only begotten Son to rule us, and hast by thy good pleasure consecrated him a King over us, that we may be perpetually safe and secure under his hand against all the attempts of the devil and of the whole world, - O grant, that we may suffer ourselves to be ruled by his authority, and so conduct ourselves, that he may ever continue to watch for our safety: and as thou hast committed us to him, that he may be the guardian of our salvation, so also suffer us not either to turn aside or to fall, but preserve us ever in his service, until we be at length gathered into that blessed and everlasting kingdom, which has been procured for us by the blood of thy only Son. Amen.

Psalm 100

All people that on earth do dwell,
Sing to the Lord with cheerful voice.
Him serve with mirth, his praise forth tell,
Come ye before him and rejoice.
Know that the Lord is God indeed;
Without our aid he did us make:
We are his flock, he doth us feed,
And for his sheep he doth us take.

O enter then his gates with praise,
Approach with joy his courts unto:
Praise, laud, and bless his name always,
For it is seemly so to do.
For why? the Lord our God is good,
His mercy is for ever sure;
His truth at all times firmly stood,
And shall from age to age endure.

Monday: Grant, Almighty God, that as we now carry about us this mortal body, yea, and nourish through sin a thousand deaths within us, - O grant, that we may ever by faith direct our eyes towards heaven, and to that incomprehensible power, which is to be manifested at the last day by Jesus Christ our Lord, so that in the midst of death we may hope that thou wilt be our Redeemer, and enjoy that redemption, which he completed when he rose from the dead; and not doubt but that the fruit which he then brought forth by his Spirit will come also to us, when Christ himself shall come to judge the world; and may we thus walk in the fear of thy name, that we may be really gathered among his members, to be made partakers of that glory, which by his death he has procured for us. Amen.

Psalm 13

How long wilt thou forget me, Lord?
shall it for ever be?
O how long shall it be that thou
wilt hide thy face from me?

How long take counsel in my soul,
still sad in heart, shall I?
How long exalted over me
shall be mine enemy?

O Lord my God, consider well,
and answer to me make:
Mine eyes enlighten, lest the sleep
of death me overtake:

Lest that mine enemy should say,
Against him I prevailed;
And those that trouble me rejoice,
when I am moved and failed.

But I have all my confidence
thy mercy set upon;
My heart within me shall rejoice
in thy salvation.

I will unto the Lord my God
sing praises cheerfully,
Because he hath his bounty shown
to me abundantly.

Tuesday: Grant, Almighty God, that as thou hast once appeared in the person of thy only-begotten Son, and hast rendered in him thy glory visible to us, and as thou dost daily set forth to us the same Christ in the glass of thy gospel, - O grant, that we, fixing our eyes on him, may not go astray, nor be led here and there after wicked inventions, the fallacies of Satan, and the allurements of this world: but may we continue firm in the obedience of faith and persevere in it through the whole course of our life, until we be at length fully transformed into the image of thy eternal glory, which now in part shines in us, through the same Christ our Lord. Amen.

Psalm 42

Like as the hart for water-brooks : in thirst doth pant and bray;
So pants my longing soul, O God, that come to thee I may.
My soul for God, the living God, doth thirst: when shall I near
Unto thy countenance approach, and in God's sight appear?
My tears have unto me been meat, both in the night and day,
While unto me continually, Where is thy God? they say.

My soul is pourèd out in me, when this I think upon;
Because that with the multitude : I heretofore had gone:
With them into God's house I went, with voice of joy and praise;
Yea, with the multitude that kept : the solemn holy days.

O why art thou cast down, my soul? why in me so dismayed?
Trust God, for I shall praise him yet, his count'nance is mine aid.
My God, my soul's cast down in me; thee therefore mind I will
From Jordan's land, the Hermonites, and ev'n from Mizar hill.

At the noise of thy water-spouts : deep unto deep doth call;
Thy breaking waves pass over me, Yea, and thy billows all.
His loving-kindness yet the Lord : command will in the day,
Is song's with me by night; to God, By whom I live, I'll pray:

And I will say to God my rock, Why me forgett'st thou so?
Why, for my foes' oppression, thus mourning do I go?
'Tis as a sword within my bones, when my foes me upbraid;
Ev'n when by them, Where is thy God? 'tis daily to me said.

O why art thou cast down, my soul? why, thus with grief oppresed,
Art thou disquieted in me? in God still hope and rest:
For yet I know I shall him praise, who graciously to me
The health is of my countenance, yea, mine own God is he.

Wednesday: Grant, Almighty God, that as thou dost so kindly call on us daily by thy voice, meekly and calmly to offer ourselves to be ruled by thee, and since thou hast exalted us to a high degree of honour by freeing us from the dread of the devil, and from that tyranny which kept us in miserable fear, and hast also favoured us with the Spirit of adoption and of hope, - O grant, that we, being mindful of these benefits, may ever submit ourselves to thee, and desire only to raise our voice for this end, that the whole world may submit itself to thee, and that those who seem now to rage against thee may at length be brought, as well as we, to render thee obedience, so that thy Son Christ may be the Lord of all, to the end that thou alone mayest be exalted, and that we may be made subject to thee, and be at length raised up above, and become partakers of that glory which has been obtained for us by Christ our Lord. Amen.

Psalm 23

The Lord's my shepherd, I'll not want.
He makes me down to lie
In pastures green he leadeth me
the quiet waters by.

My soul he doth restore again;
and me to walk doth make
Within the paths of righteousness,
ev'n for his own name's sake.

Yea, though I walk in death's dark vale,
yet will I fear none ill:
For thou art with me; and thy rod
and staff me comfort still.

My table thou hast furnished
in presence of my foes;
My head thou dost with oil anoint,
and my cup overflows.

Goodness and mercy all my life
shall surely follow me:
And in God's house for evermore
my dwelling-place shall be.

Thursday: Grant, Almighty God, that as thou often dost justly hide thy face from us, so that on every side we see nothing but evidences of thy dreadful judgment, - O grant, that we, with minds raised above the scene of this world, may at the same time cherish the hope which thou constantly settest before us, so that we may feel fully persuaded that we are loved by thee, however severely thou mayest chastise us and may this consolation so support and sustain our souls, that patiently enduring whatever chastisements thou mayest lay upon us, we may ever hold fast the reconciliation which thou hast promised to us in Christ thy Son. Amen.

Psalm 121

I to the hills will lift mine eyes,
from whence doth come mine aid.
My safety cometh from the Lord,
who heav'n and earth hath made.

Thy foot he'll not let slide, nor will
he slumber that thee keeps.
Behold, he that keeps Israel,
he slumbers not, nor sleeps.

The Lord thee keeps, the Lord thy shade
on thy right hand doth stay:
The moon by night thee shall not smite,
nor yet the sun by day.

The Lord shall keep thy soul; he shall
preserve thee from all ill.
Henceforth thy going out and in
God keep for ever will.

Friday: Grant, Almighty God, that as we are in this life subject to so many miseries, and in the meantime grow insensible in our sins, - O grant that we may learn to search ourselves and consider one sins, that we may be really humbled before thee, and ascribe to ourselves the blame of all our evils, that we may be thus led to a genuine feeling of repentance, and so strive to be reconciled to thee in Christ, that we may wholly depend on thy paternal love, and thus ever aspire to the fulness of eternal felicity, through thy goodness and that immeasurable kindness which thou testifies is ready and offered to all those, who with a sincere heart worship thee, call upon thee, and flee to thee, through Christ our Lord. Amen.

Psalm 130

Lord, from the depths to thee I cried.
My voice, Lord, do thou hear:
Unto my supplication's voice
give an attentive ear.
Lord, who shall stand, if thou, O Lord,
should'st mark iniquity?
But yet with thee forgiveness is,
that feared thou mayest be.

I wait for God, my soul doth wait,
my hope is in his word.
More than they that for morning watch,
my soul waits for the Lord;
I say, more than they that do watch
the morning light to see.
Let Israel hope in the Lord,
for with him mercies be;

And plenteous redemption
is ever found with him.
And from all his iniquities
He Isr'el shall redeem.

Saturday: Grant, Almighty God, that as thou hast once adopted us, and continue to confirm this thy favour by calling us unceasingly to thyself, and dost not only severely chastise us, but also gently and paternally invite us to thyself, and exhort us at the same time to repentance, - O grant that we may not be so hardened as to resist thy goodness, nor abuse this thine incredible forbearance, but submit ourselves in obedience to thee; that whenever thou mayest severely chastise us, we may bear thy corrections with genuine submission of faith, and not continue untameable and obstinate to the last, but return to thee the only fountain of life and salvation, that as thou has once begun in us a good work, so thou mayest perfect it to the day of our Lord. Amen.

Psalm 124

Now Israel may say, and that truly,
If that the Lord had not our cause maintained;
If that the Lord had not our right sustained,
When cruel men against us furiously
Rose up in wrath, to make of us their prey;

Then certainly they had devoured us all,
And swallowed quick, for ought that we could deem;
Such was their rage, as we might well esteem.
And as fierce floods before them all things drown,
So had they brought our soul to death quite down.

The raging streams, with their proud swelling waves,
Had then our soul o'erwhelmèd in the deep.
But blessed be God, who doth us safely keep,
And hath not giv'n us for a living prey
Unto their teeth, and bloody cruelty.

Ev'n as a bird out of the fowler's snare
Escapes away, so is our soul set free:
Broke are their nets, and thus escapèd we.
Therefore our help is in the Lord's great name,
Who heav'n and earth by his great pow'r did frame.

Prayers of other Reformers

Martin Bucer (from the Strasbourg Liturgy):

Almighty, eternal God and Father, we confess and acknowledge unto You that we were conceived in unrighteousness and are full of sin and transgression in all our life. We do not fully believe Your Word nor follow Your holy commandments. Remember Your goodness, we beseech You, and for Your Name's sake be gracious unto us, and forgive us our iniquity which, alas, is great Amen.

Almighty, gracious Father, forasmuch as our whole salvation depends upon our true understanding of Your holy Word, grant to all of us that our hearts, being freed from worldly affairs, may hear and apprehend Your holy Word with all diligence and faith, that we may rightly understand Your gracious will, cherish it, and live by it with all earnestness, to Your praise and honor; through our Lord Jesus Christ. Amen.

Grant unto us, O heavenly Father, that the remembrance of our redemption may never leave our hearts, but that we may walk in Christ, the Light of the world, far removed from our foolish reason and blind wills, which are vain and injurious darkness; through Jesus Christ our Lord. Amen.

Almighty God, heavenly Father, we give You eternal praise and thanks that You have been so gracious unto us poor sinners, having drawn us to Your Son our Lord Jesus, whom You have delivered to death for us and given to be our nourishment and our dwelling unto eternal life. Grant that we may never relinquish these things from our hearts, but ever grow and increase in faith to You, which, through love, is effective of all good works. And so may our whole life be devoted to Your praise and the edification of our neighbour; through the same Jesus Christ, our Lord. Amen.

John Knox:

Omnipotent and everlasting God, Father of our Lord Jesus Christ, who by thy eternal providence disposest kingdoms as seemeth best to thy wisdom: We acknowledge and confess thy judgments to be righteous, in that thou hast taken from us, for our ingratitude, and for the abusing of thy most holy Word, our native king and Earthly comforter.

Justly mayest thou pour forth upon us the uttermost of thy plagues, for we have not known the days and time of our merciful visitation. We have scorned thy Word, and despised thy mercies; we have transgressed thy laws, for deceitfully have we wrought, every man with our neighbour; oppression and violence we have not abhorred; charity hath not appeared among us, as our profession requires. We have little regarded the voices of thy prophets. Thy threatenings we have believed to be vanity and wind. So that in us, of ourselves, there remains nothing worthy of thy mercy, for all are found fruitless; even the princes with the prophets, as withered trees apt and meet to be burned in the fire of thy eternal displeasure.

But, O Lord, behold thy own mercy and goodness, that thou mayest purge and remove the burden of our most horrible offenses. Let thy love overcome the severity of thy judgments, even as it did in giving to the world thy only Son, Jesus, when all mankind was lost, and no obedience was left in Adam or in his seed. Regenerate our hearts, O Lord, by the strength of the Holy Spirit. Convert thou us, and we shall be converted.

Work thou in us unfeigned repentance, and move thou our hearts to obey thy holy laws. Take not from us the light of thy gospel. Repress thou the pride of those that would rebel; and remove from all hearts the contempt of thy Word. Look thou to the honor of thy own name, O Lord; and let thy gospel be preached with boldness in this realm. If thy justice must punish, then punish our bodies with the rod of thy mercy and let us not faint under the cross of our Saviour, but assist us with the Holy Spirit, even to the end.
Amen.

The Book of Common Prayer

Produced in various editions from 1549, chiefly edited by the English reformer and martyr Thomas Cranmer (1489-1556). These prayers come from the 1662 edition.

Morning Prayer

Confession: Almighty and most merciful Father, we have erred, and strayed from thy ways like lost sheep. We have followed too much the devices and desires of our own hearts. We have offended against thy holy laws. We have left undone those things which we ought to have done; and we have done those things which we ought not to have done; and there is no health in us. But thou, O Lord, have mercy upon us, miserable offenders. Spare thou them, O God, which confess their faults. Restore thou them that are penitent; according to thy promises declared unto mankind in Christ Jesu our Lord. And grant, O most merciful Father, for his sake, that we may hereafter live a godly, righteous, and sober life, to the glory of thy holy name. Amen.

Lord's Prayer: Our Father, which art in heaven, hallowed be thy name; thy kingdom come; thy will be done, in earth as it is in heaven. Give us this day our daily bread. And forgive us our trespasses, as we forgive them that trespass against us. And lead us not into temptation; but deliver us from evil. For thine is the kingdom, the power and the glory, for ever and ever. Amen.

Apostles' Creed: I Believe in God the Father Almighty, Maker of heaven and earth: And in Jesus Christ his only Son our Lord: Who was conceived by the Holy Ghost, Born of the Virgin Mary: Suffered under Pontius Pilate, Was crucified, dead, and buried: He descended into hell; The third day he rose again from the dead: He ascended into heaven, And sitteth on the right hand of God the Father Almighty: From thence he shall come to judge the quick and the dead. I believe in the Holy Ghost: The holy Catholic Church; The Communion of Saints: The Forgiveness of sins: The Resurrection of the body: And the Life everlasting. Amen.

Te Deum: We praise thee, O God; we acknowledge thee to be the Lord. All the earth doth worship thee, the Father everlasting.
To thee all angels cry aloud, the heavens and all the powers therein.
To thee cherubin and seraphin continually do cry,
Holy, Holy, Holy, Lord God of Sabaoth; Heaven and earth are full of the majesty of thy glory.
The glorious company of the apostles praise thee.
The goodly fellowship of the prophets praise thee.
The noble army of martyrs praise thee.

The holy Church throughout all the world doth acknowledge thee: the Father of an infinite majesty; thine honourable, true and only Son; also the Holy Ghost the Comforter.

Thou art the King of glory, O Christ.
Thou art the everlasting Son of the Father.
When thou tookest upon thee to deliver man, thou didst not abhor the Virgin's womb.
When thou hadst overcome the sharpness of death, thou didst open the kingdom of heaven to all believers.
Thou sittest at the right hand of God, in the glory of the Father.
We believe that thou shalt come to be our judge.
We therefore pray thee, help thy servants, whom thou hast redeemed with thy precious blood.
Make them to be numbered with thy saints in glory everlasting.

O Lord, save thy people and bless thine heritage.
Govern them and lift them up for ever.
Day by day we magnify thee; and we worship thy name, ever world without end.
Vouchsafe, O Lord, to keep us this day without sin.
O Lord, have mercy upon us, have mercy upon us.
O Lord, let thy mercy lighten upon us, as our trust is in thee.
O Lord, in thee have I trusted; let me never be confounded.

Kyrie: Lord, have mercy upon us.
Christ, have mercy upon us.
Lord, have mercy upon us.

Collect for Peace: O God, who art the author of peace and lover of concord, in knowledge of whom standeth our eternal life, whose service is perfect freedom; defend us thy humble servants in all assaults of our enemies; that we, surely trusting in thy defence, may not fear the power of any adversaries; through the might of Jesus Christ our Lord. Amen.

Collect for Grace: O Lord, our heavenly Father, almighty and everlasting God, who hast safely brought us to the beginning of this day; defend us in the same with thy mighty power; and grant that this day we fall into no sin, neither run into any kind of danger, but that all our doings may be ordered by thy governance, to do always that is righteous in thy sight; through Jesus Christ our Lord. Amen.

Grace: The grace of our Lord Jesus Christ, and the love of God, and the fellowship of the Holy Ghost, be with us all evermore. Amen. (2 Corinthians 13.)

Evening Prayer

Confession: Almighty and most merciful Father, we have erred, and strayed from thy ways like lost sheep. We have followed too much the devices and desires of our own hearts. We have offended against thy holy laws. We have left undone those things which we ought to have done; and we have done those things which we ought not to have done; and there is no health in us. But thou, O Lord, have mercy upon us, miserable offenders. Spare thou them, O God, which confess their faults. Restore thou them that are penitent; according to thy promises declared unto mankind in Christ Jesu our Lord. And grant, O most merciful Father, for his sake, that we may hereafter live a godly, righteous, and sober life, to the glory of thy holy name. Amen.

Lord's Prayer: Our Father, which art in heaven, hallowed be thy name; thy kingdom come; thy will be done, in earth as it is in heaven. Give us this day our daily bread. And forgive us our trespasses, as we forgive them that trespass against us. And lead us not into temptation; but deliver us from evil. For thine is the kingdom, the power and the glory, for ever and ever. Amen.

Magnificat: My soul doth magnify the Lord, and my spirit hath rejoiced in God my Saviour.
For he hath regarded the lowliness of his handmaiden.
For behold, from henceforth all generations shall call me blessed.
For he that is mighty hath magnified me; and holy is his Name.
And his mercy is on them that fear him throughout all generations.
He hath showed strength with his arm; he hath scattered the proud in the imagination of their hearts.
He hath put down the mighty from their seat, and hath exalted the humble and meek.
He hath filled the hungry with good things; and the rich he hath sent empty away.
He remembering his mercy hath holpen his servant Israel; as he promised to our forefathers, Abraham and his seed, for ever.
Glory be to the Father, and to the Son and to the Holy Ghost; As it was in the beginning, is now, and ever shall be world without end. Amen. (Luke 1. 46)

Nunc Dimittis: Lord, now lettest thou thy servant depart in peace, according to thy word. For mine eyes have seen thy salvation, Which thou hast prepared before the face of all people; To be a light to lighten the Gentiles and to be the glory of thy people Israel. Glory be to the Father, and to the Son and to the Holy Ghost; As it was in the beginning, is now, and ever shall be world without end. Amen. (Luke 2.29)

Apostles' Creed: I Believe in God the Father Almighty, Maker of heaven and earth: And in Jesus Christ his only Son our Lord: Who was conceived by the Holy Ghost, Born of the Virgin Mary: Suffered under Pontius Pilate, Was crucified, dead, and buried: He descended into hell; The third day he rose again from the dead: He ascended into heaven, And sitteth on the right hand of God the Father Almighty: From thence he shall come to judge the quick and the dead. I believe in the Holy Ghost: The holy Catholic Church; The Communion of Saints: The Forgiveness of sins: The Resurrection of the body: And the Life everlasting. Amen.

Kyrie: Lord, have mercy upon us.
            Christ, have mercy upon us.
            Lord, have mercy upon us.

Collect for Peace: O God, from whom all holy desires, all good counsels, and all just works do proceed; Give unto thy servants that peace which the world cannot give; that our hearts may be set to obey thy commandments, and also that by thee, we, being defended from the fear of our enemies, may pass our time in rest and quietness; through the merits of Jesus Christ our Saviour. Amen.

Collect for Aid against all Perils: Lighten our darkness, we beseech thee, O Lord; and by thy great mercy defend us from all perils and dangers of this night; for the love of thy only Son, our Saviour, Jesus Christ. Amen.

Grace: The grace of our Lord Jesus Christ, and the love of God, and the fellowship of the Holy Ghost, be with us all evermore. Amen. (2 Corinthians 13.)

Night Prayer (Compline)

The Lord almighty grant us a quiet night and a perfect end.

Into thy hands, O Lord, I commend my spirit. For thou hast redeemed me, O Lord, thou God of truth. Keep me as the apple of an eye. Hide me under the shadow of thy wings.

Preserve us, O Lord, while waking, and guard us while sleeping, that awake we may watch with Christ, and asleep we may rest in peace. Visit, we beseech thee, O Lord, this place, and drive from it all the snares of the enemy; let thy holy angels dwell herein to preserve us in peace; and may thy blessing be upon us evermore; through Jesus Christ our Lord. Amen.

O Lord Jesus Christ, Son of the Living God, who at this evening hour didst rest in the sepulchre, and didst thereby sanctify the grave to be a bed of hope to thy people: make us so to abound in sorrow for our sins, which were the cause of thy passion, that when our bodies lie in the dust, our souls may live with thee: who livest and reignest with the Father and the Holy Spirit, one God world without end. Amen.

Look down, O Lord, from thy heavenly throne, illuminate the darkness of this night with thy celestial brightness, and from the children of light banish the deeds of darkness; through Jesus Christ our Lord. Amen.

Be present, O merciful God, and protect us through the silent hours of this night, so that we who are wearied by the changes and chances of this fleeting world, may repose upon thy eternal changelessness; through Jesus Christ our Lord.

Abide with us, O Lord, for it is toward evening and the day is far spent. As the watchmen look for the morning, so do we look for thee, O Christ. The almighty and merciful Lord, the Father, the Son and the Holy Ghost, bless us and preserve us. Amen.

Common Prayer & Psalms for a Week

Sunday: Almighty God, Father of all mercies, we thine unworthy servants do give thee most humble and hearty thanks for all thy goodness and loving-kindness to us and to all men; We bless thee for our creation, preservation, and all the blessings of this life; but above all for thine inestimable love in the redemption of the world by our Lord Jesus Christ, for the means of grace, and for the hope of glory. And we beseech thee, give us that due sense of all thy mercies, that our hearts may be unfeignedly thankful, and that we shew forth thy praise, not only with our lips, but in our lives; by giving up ourselves to thy service, and by walking before thee in holiness and righteousness all our days; through Jesus Christ our Lord, to whom with thee and the Holy Ghost be all honour and glory, world without end. Amen.

Venite (Psalm 95): O come, let us sing unto the Lord : let us heartily rejoice in the strength of our salvation.
Let us come before his presence with thanksgiving : and show ourselves glad in him with psalms.
For the Lord is a great God: and a great King above all gods. In his hand are all the corners of the earth : and the strength of the hills is his also.
The sea is his, and he made it : and his hands prepared the dry land.
O come, let us worship and fall down : and kneel before the Lord our Maker. For he is the Lord our God : and we are the people of his pasture, and the sheep of his hand.
To day if ye will hear his voice, harden not your hearts : as in the provocation, and as in the day of temptation in the wilderness; When your fathers tempted me : proved me, and saw my works.
Forty years long was I grieved with this generation, and said : It is a people that do err in their hearts, for they have not known my ways. Unto whom I sware in my wrath : that they should not enter into my rest.

Monday: Almighty God, unto whom all hearts be open, all desires known, and from whom no secrets are hid: Cleanse the thoughts of our hearts by the inspiration of thy Holy Spirit, that we may perfectly love thee, and worthily magnify thy holy Name; through Christ our Lord. Amen.

Jubilate (Psalm 100): O be joyful in the Lord, all ye lands : serve the Lord with gladness, and come before his presence with a song.
Be ye sure that the Lord he is God : it is he that hath made us, and not we ourselves; we are his people, and the sheep of his pasture.
O go your way into his gates with thanksgiving, and into his courts with praise : be thankful unto him, and speak good of his Name.
For the Lord is gracious, his mercy is everlasting : and his truth endureth from generation to generation.

Tuesday: O God, merciful Father, that despisest not the sighing of a contrite heart, nor the desire of such as be sorrowful: Mercifully assist our prayers that we make before thee in all our troubles and adversities, whensoever they oppress us; and graciously hear us, that those evils, which the craft and subtilty of the devil or man worketh against us, be brought to nought, and by the providence of thy goodness they may be dispersed; that we thy servants, being hurt by no persecutions, may evermore give thanks unto thee in thy holy Church; through Jesus Christ our Lord.

Deus misereatur (Psalm 67): God be merciful unto us, and bless us, and show us tile light of his countenance, and be merciful unto us;
That thy way may be known upon earth, thy saving health among all nations.
Let the people praise thee, O God; yea, let all the people praise thee.
O let the nations rejoice and be glad; for thou shalt judge the folk righteously, and govern the nations upon earth.
Let the people praise thee, O God; yea, let all the people praise thee.
Then shall the earth bring forth her increase; and God, even our own God, shall give us his blessing.
God shall bless us; and all the ends of the world shall fear him.

Wednesday: Prevent us, O Lord, in all our doings with thy most gracious favour, and further us with thy continual help; that in all our works begun, continued, and ended in thee, we may glorify thy holy Name, and finally by thy mercy obtain everlasting life; through Jesus Christ our Lord.

Benedic, anima mea (Psalm 103): Praise the Lord, O my soul; and all that is within me, praise his holy Name.
Praise the Lord, O my soul, and forget not all his benefits:
Who forgiveth all thy sin, and healeth all thine infirmities;
Who saveth thy life from destruction, and crowneth thee with mercy and loving-kindness.
O praise the Lord, ye angels of his, ye that excel in strength; * ye that fulfill his commandment, and hearken unto the voice of his word.
O praise the Lord, all ye his hosts; ye servants of his that do his pleasure.
O speak good of the Lord, all ye works of his, in all places of his dominion: praise thou the Lord, O my soul.

Thursday: O God, the Creator and Preserver of all mankind, we humbly beseech thee for all sorts and conditions of men; that thou wouldest be pleased to make thy ways known unto them, thy saving health unto all nations. More especially we pray for the good estate of the Catholic Church; that it may be so guided and governed by thy good Spirit, that all who profess and call themselves Christians may be led into the way of truth, and hold the faith in unity of spirit, in the bond of peace, and in righteousness of life. Finally we commend to thy fatherly goodness all those, who are any ways afflicted or distressed in mind, body, or estate; that it may please thee to comfort and relieve them, according to their several necessities giving them patience under their sufferings, and a happy issue out of all their afflictions. And this we beg for Jesus Christ his sake. Amen.

In te, Domine, speravi (Psalm 31. 1-6): In thee, O Lord, have I put my trust : let me never be put to confusion, deliver me in thy righteousness. Bow down thine ear to me : make haste to deliver me. And be thou my strong rock, and house of defence : that thou mayest save me. For thou art my strong rock, and my castle : be thou also my guide, and lead me for thy Name's sake. Draw me out of the net, that they have laid privily for me : for thou art my strength. Into thy hands I commend my spirit : for thou hast redeemed me, O Lord, thou God of truth.

Friday: We humbly beseech thee, O Father, mercifully to look upon our infirmities; and for the glory of thy Name turn from us all those evils that we most righteously have deserved; and grant that in all our troubles we may put our whole trust and confidence in thy mercy, and evermore serve thee in holiness and pureness of living, to thy honour and glory; through our only Mediator and Advocate, Jesus Christ our Lord. Amen.

Confitebor tibi (Psalm 111): I will give thanks unto the Lord with my whole heart, secretly among the faithful, and in the congregation.
The works of the Lord are great, sought out of all them that have pleasure therein.
His work is worthy to be praised and had in honour, and his righteousness endureth for ever.
The merciful and gracious Lord hath so done his marvellous works, that they ought to be had in remembrance.
He hath given meat unto them that fear him; he shall ever be mindful of his covenant.
He hath showed his people the power of his works, that he may give them the heritage of the heathen.
The works of his hands are verity and judgment; all his commandments are true.
They stand fast for ever and ever, and are done in truth and equity.
He sent redemption unto his people; he hath commanded his covenant for ever; holy and reverend is his Name.
The fear of the Lord is the beginning of wisdom; a good understanding have all they that do thereafter; his praise endureth for ever.

Saturday: O almighty Lord, and everlasting God, vouchsafe, we beseech thee, to direct, sanctify, and govern, both our hearts and bodies, in the ways of thy laws, and in the works of thy commandments; that through thy most mighty protection, both here and ever, we may be preserved in body and soul; through our Lord and Saviour Jesus Christ. Amen.

Confitemini Domino (Psalm 107 1-9): O give thanks unto the Lord, for he is gracious, and his mercy endureth for ever.
Let them give thanks whom the Lord hath redeemed and delivered from the hand of the enemy;
And gathered them out of the lands, from the east, and from the west; from the north, and from the south.
They went astray in the wilderness out of the way, and found no city to dwell in. Hungry and thirsty, their soul fainted in them.
So they cried unto the Lord in their trouble, and he delivered them from their distress. He led them forth by the right way, that they might go to the city where they dwelt.
O that men would therefore praise the Lord for his goodness; and declare the wonders that he doeth for the children of men!
For he satisfieth the empty soul, and filleth the hungry soul with goodness.

Scripture Sentences

- WHEN the wicked man turneth away from his wickedness that he hath committed, and doeth that which is lawful and right, he shall save his soul alive. Ez 18.27

- I acknowledge my transgressions, and my sin is ever before me. Ps 51.3

- The sacrifices of God are a broken spirit : a broken and a contrite heart, O God, thou wilt not despise. Ps 51.17

- Rend your heart, and not your garments, and turn unto the Lord your God: for he is gracious and merciful, slow to anger, and of great kindness, and repenteth him of the evil. Joel 2.13

- If we say that we have no sin, we deceive ourselves, and the truth is not in us: but if we confess our sins, he is faithful and just to forgive us our sins, and to cleanse us from all unrighteousness. 1 John 1.8-9

- So God loved the world, that he gave his only-begotten Son, to the end that all that believe in him should not perish, but have everlasting life. John 3.16

- This is a true saying, and worthy of all men to be received, that Christ Jesus came into the world to save sinners. 1 Timothy 1.15

- Be sober, be vigilant; because your adversary the devil, as a roaring lion, walketh about, seeking whom he may devour: whom resist, steadfast in the faith: 1 Peter 5.8,9

- Come unto me, all ye that labour and are heavy laden, and I will give you rest. Take my yoke upon you, and learn of me; for I am meek and lowly in heart: and ye shall find rest unto your souls. For my yoke is easy, and my burden is light. Matt 11.28-30

John Habermann: The Christian's Companion

Morning and Evening Prayers for All Days of the Week
Together With Confessional, Communion, and Other Prayers
and Hymns for Mornings and Evenings, and Other Occasions
By Johann Habermann (1516-90, German Reformer)

Morning & Evening Prayers for a Week

Prayer for Sunday Morning.

Lord, our Heavenly Father, Eternal God! Blessed be Thy divine power and might; magnified Thy fathomless goodness and mercy; praised Thine eternal wisdom and truth. For Thou hast shielded me with Thy hand against the perils of this night, and hast suffered me to rest and slumber in peace under the shadow of Thy wings. Thou hast kept and safeguarded me with a father's care against the Evil One and all his wicked designs and purposes. Therefore, I magnify Thy goodness and the wonders which Thou doest for the children of men. I will exalt Thee in the congregation. Thy praise shall evermore be in my mouth. My soul shall bless Thee, O my Lord, all that is within me shall bless Thy holy name, and nevermore will I forget Thy benefits. May the praises of my lips, which in singleness of heart I bring before Thee at this early hour, be acceptable in Thy sight. I call upon Thee with all my heart to preserve me this day against all danger of body and soul. May Thy holy angels have charge over me and keep me in all my ways. Encompass me with Thy shield and lead me on the paths of Thy commandments that, like the children of light, I may be blameless in Thy service, to Thy good pleasure. Stay the Evil One and all wickedness of this world. Restrain mine own flesh and blood that I be not overcome by them. Lead me with Thy Holy Spirit that I attempt, do, speak, or think nothing except what is well-pleasing in Thy sight and conducive to the glory of Thy divine Majesty. Behold, O God, I consecrate and dedicate myself entirely to Thy holy will, with body and soul, all my powers and abilities, inwardly and outwardly. Make me a living sacrifice, holy and acceptable unto Thee, so that I may render Thee a reasonable and pleasing service. Therefore, Most Holy Father, Almighty God, let me be wholly Thine. Govern Thou my heart and soul, and all my emotions that I know and understand none but Thee. O Lord, in the morning wilt Thou hear my voice. Early will I seek Thee and look up to Thee. Early will I praise Thee, and will not cease when evening comes. Through Jesus Christ. Amen.

Gott des Himmels und der Erden.

God, Who madest earth and heaven,—
Father, Son, and Holy Ghost,
Who the day and night hast given,
Sun and moon, and starry host,
Thou Whose mighty hand sustains
Earth and all that it contains;

Praise to Thee my soul shall render,
Who this night has guarded me,
My omnipotent Defender,
Who from ill doth set me free;
Free from danger, anguish, woe,
Free from the infernal foe.

Let the night of my transgression
With night's darkness pass away;
Jesus, into Thy possession
I resign myself to-day.
In Thy wounds I find relief
From my greatest sin and grief.

Let my life and conversation
Be directed by Thy Word;
Lord, Thy constant preservation
To Thy erring child afford.
Nowhere but alone in Thee
From all harm can I be free.

Wholly to Thy blest protection
I commit my heart and mind;
Mighty God! to Thy direction
Wholly may I be resigned.
Lord, my Shield, my Light divine,
O accept, and own me Thine.

Heinrich Albert, 1643. Tr. John Christian Jacobi, 1720, Arthur Tozer
Russell, 1848, Catherine Winkworth, 1855.

Prayer for Sunday Evening.

Eternal God, Merciful Father, I lift up my hands unto Thee as an evening sacrifice, and render Thee most hearty thanks, praise, and glory, that Thou hast protected me this day and all the days of my life from all evil and calamity, and through the ministrations of Thy holy angels hast graciously guarded me against the Evil One. I pray Thee to forgive me all my sins, wherever I have done wrong. Surround me this night with Thy holy angels. May thou compass me round and cast a trench about me, that I may escape the snares and evil cunning of the enemy. I commend myself to Thy goodness and mercy. Protect me with Thine outstretched arm; for from my heart do I pant after Thee in the nightwatches, and with my spirit within me do I watch for Thee at all times. I wait upon Thy goodness, and my soul trusts in Thee, the living God, for Thou art my refuge and my Saviour. Behold, O Lord, whether we sleep or wake, we are Thine: whether we live or die, Thou art our God who hast called us into being. Therefore, I cry unto Thee: let Thy grace be not far from me. Shelter me with Thy shield. Keep me, that I lie in quiet, sleep in peace, and awake again in health. Hide me in Thy pavilion in the time of trouble, in the secret of Thy tabernacle hide me, set me upon the rock, and I will fear no evil. Yea, though I walk through the valley of the shadow of death, I will fear no evil: for Thou art with me; Thy rod and Thy staff they comfort me. Grant me grace, that though my body sleep, my soul may ever wake for Thee, that I may ever have Thee in my heart and before my mind, and be not overcome by the night of sin. Keep me from all wicked and evil dreams, from restless wakings and useless anxieties, from depraved and hurtful thoughts, from all grief. My Lord and God, into Thy gracious care do I commend my body and soul, my brothers and sisters, and all my kin and loved ones. May it please Thee, O Lord, to save us, and turn not Thy mercy from us. May Thy grace and fidelity protect us alway. Cover us this night with Thy goodness, and encompass us with Thy mercy, that we be safe-guarded in body and soul. Amen.

Christe, du bist der helle Tag.

O Christ, who art the sun-lit day,
Before Thee night must flee away,
Thou dost reflect the Father's light
And teachest us His will aright.

Dear Lord, as night is drawing near,
Fill Thou our hearts with light and cheer,
Let us securely rest in Thee
And from the foe's attacks stay free.

And while our eyes in slumber close,
Grant that our hearts may find repose;
But let them be to Thee awake
And of Thy saving grace partake.

Protect us from the wily foe
Who seeks to harm our souls, we know.
Be Thou our shield, our staff, and stay,
Lord Jesus Christ, for this we pray.

For Thou hast made us, Lord, Thine own,
We as Thy heritage are known.
Thy blood was shed, that we might be
The Father's precious gift to Thee.

So let Thy holy angel stay
Around us both by night and day.
Place Thou a watch beside our bed,
And guardian angels overhead.

Thus in Thy name we fall asleep,
While angels o'er us watch must keep.
To Thee, O Holy One in Three,
Be praise to all eternity.

Latin, 7 Century, Erasmus Alber, 1555, Tr. H. Brueckner, 1918.

Prayer for Monday Morning.

O Thou Eternal and Merciful God! Thou hast commanded Thy people in Thy law each morning to offer Thee a burnt offering, thereby to praise and thank Thee for Thy merciful protection: thus I too would bring unto Thee my offering of praise, that is the fruit of my lips, and magnify Thy holy name. For by Thy grace and mercy Thou hast kept me this night from all evil and harm in body and soul, and hast graciously protected me. If Thou hadst not been my shield and my help, manifold calamities would have engulfed me, and I could not have risen in health and safety. Therefore, I thank Thee for Thy protection.

But I continue to call to Thee from the depths of my heart, and my supplication ascends to Thee in the early hour. Early do I seek Thy countenance and pray Thee to safeguard me and mine from the wiles and power of the devil, from sin and disgrace and all wickedness. Visit Thou me in this early hour with Thy grace, as without Thee I can do nothing, and grant that I may this day begin all my work in Thy name and end it joyously, to the glory of Thy divine majesty and the betterment of my neighbour.

Preserve my soul, mind, reason, senses, and thoughts, all that I do and leave undone, that the prince of darkness do me no injury. Safeguard me against the destruction that wasteth at noonday. Defend me against mine enemies that neither secretly nor openly they harm or injure me with their craft and cunning, violence or malice.

O God, Father and Lord of my life, shield me from all impurity and disorderly conduct. Keep me from all intemperance and unchastity, and turn from me shameless thoughts. Help me by Thy grace to pluck out the eye that offends me and cast it away, and renounce all wicked and impure desires of the heart. Grant whatever is pleasing to Thee and useful to me, that I may serve Thee in the true faith.

Look upon me with the eyes of Thy mercy, Thou Saviour of the world, and enlighten my heart and eyes, that I may walk in the light of Thy grace, which rises above me, and never lose Thee, the Eternal Light. Amen.

Ach bleib mit deiner Gnade.

Abide with grace unbounded,
Lord Jesus, with us still,
That Satan's craft confounded
May no more work us ill.

Abide with us, dear Saviour,
Both with and in Thy Word:
To us both now and ever
Thy saving health afford.

Abide with all Thy brightness,
Thou brightest Light of all;
And lest we stray from rightness,
Make Thou Thy truth our wall.

Abide with us and bless us,
Thou Lord whose riches 'bide;
With growing grace possess us
And all things best provide.

Abide with Thy protection,
Great Captain, clothed with might;
O'ercome our world affection
And vanquish Satan's spite.

Abide with care untiring,
Our God and Lord indeed;
All steadfastness inspiring,
Help, Lord, our every need.

Josua Stegmann, 1630, Tr. A. Ramsey, 1916.

Prayer for Monday Evening.

O Thou Mighty and Everlasting God, the Father of our Lord Jesus Christ, I thank Thee that by Thy divine power Thou hast this day preserved me from all injury and danger of body and life. I owe it to Thy mercy alone that Thou didst protect me on all my paths. I pray Thee to forgive me all my sins which I have committed against Thee, and this night and during our entire lives mercifully to defend me and my loved ones against all sorrow and anxiety, and against the craft and power of the devil, wherewith day and night he seeks to ensnare us. Preserve us from the deadly pestilence that walketh in the darkness, and deliver us from the snare of the enemy. Protect us from the temptation and terror of Satan, from all evils of body and soul. For Thou art our strong fortress, our sword and buckler. All our hope and trust rests in Thee.
Therefore, O faithful God, may Thine eyes be upon us and we be safeguarded this night against all violence and assault of the enemy. Be Thou our keeper and protector. Encompass us with Thy shelter, for in Thee is our salvation. Unto Thee only, from whom cometh my help, do I lift up mine eyes. My help cometh from the Lord, who made heaven and earth.
Behold, as the eyes of servants look unto the hands of their masters, and as the eyes of a maiden unto the hand of her mistress; so our eyes wait upon the Lord our God, until that He have mercy upon us. Have mercy upon us, O Lord, have mercy, for we are poor and needy. Lift upon me the light of Thy countenance lest I sleep the sleep of death. Amen.

Nun ruhen alle Waelder.

Now under night's dark shadow Rest woodland, field, and meadow,
The world in slumber lies.
But thou, my soul, awake thee, To song and prayer betake thee,
Give praise to Him who rules the skies.

The sun's fair light hath vanished, The night its rays hath banished,
The night, the foe of day.
'Tis well: my heart containeth A sun whose light ne'er waneth,
Since Jesus there holds constant sway.

The reign of day is over, And golden stars now cover
The canopy so blue.
Thus I shall shine in heaven, Where golden crowns are given
To all who faithful stay and true.

My body is divested Of garments that have rested
Upon its form of clay.
Thus I at heaven's portal Shall lose all that is mortal
And with the Lord forever stay.

Head, feet, and hands are taking Sweet rest from toil and waking,
Released from ev'ry pain.
O heart of mine, why borrow The troubles of tomorrow?
Thou rest from sin and woe shalt gain.

Ye members weak and tired, By joy no more inspired,
Betake yourselves to bed.
The time and hour for sleeping In God's own faithful keeping
Will come when you are cold and dead.

My tired eyes are closing, And while I am reposing,
Where doth my soul remain?
To Thee be it commended Until the night is ended,
Let me Thy gracious favor gain.

Lord Jesus, who dost love me, Spread both Thy wings above me,
Thus shielding me from harm.
If Satan should draw near me, Let angels come to cheer me
And so the wily foe disarm.

My loved ones, rest securely, Since God will guard you surely
From pain and perils sore.
May you in safety slumber, While angels without number
Attend you now and evermore.

Paul Gerhardt, 1648, Tr. H. Brueckner, 1918.

Prayer for Tuesday Morning.

Blessed be God, the maker of heaven and earth, blessed be the Lord, who only doeth wondrous things, and blessed be His glorious name for ever who hath made both day and night through His glorious wisdom, and so ruled, that while the earth remaineth, they shall not cease, that man may rest by night, and proceed again to his Labours by day. O Lord, how manifold are Thy works! In wisdom hast Thou made them all: the earth is full of Thy riches. For such Thy gifts we should thank Thee ere the sun rises, and come into Thy presence when the light breaks forth. Therefore I bless Thee now also, for Thou hast suffered me securely to rest and sleep this night, and again awakened me to the joy of living. Thou hast mercifully sheltered me from the assaults and malice of enemies.
I supplicate Thy grace: grant that my soul may repose in Thy hands, my body continue in health according to Thy good pleasure, and be kept from all injury and peril. Be Thou my mighty protection and strong stay, a defence from heat, and my cover from the sun at noon, my preservation from stumbling, and my help from falling, that no harm may come unto me. O Merciful God, knowing the hour is come to awaken out of the sleep of sin and iniquity, for now is our salvation so near, the night is far spent, the day is at hand: so help us to cast off the works of darkness, and put on the armour of light, that we may walk honestly as in the day; not in rioting and drunkenness, not in chambering and wantonness, not in strife and envying, but putting on the Lord Jesus Christ in the true faith and a Christian conduct. Thus awaken us each morning.
Open Thou my ears that I may hear Thy holy Word with a believing heart and keep the same in my memory. Let my ears incline to the entreaties and prayers of the needy, not to forsake them in their distress. And when in my distress I cry unto Thee, hear Thou the voice of my supplications, and despise not my sighings in the hour of death. Let my prayers come before Thee early. Incline Thine ears to my entreaties. Satisfy us early with Thy mercy; that we may rejoice and be glad all our days. Amen.

Wach auf, mein Herz, und singe.

Awake, my heart, rejoicing,
Thy Maker's praises voicing,—
The Giver, good gifts sending;
Their Shield, His folk defending.

All night while darkness 'bound me
In deepest gloom around me,
By Satan craved while sleeping
God had me in His keeping.

Thou spak'st me words endearing;
Sleep now, my child, unfearing;
Sleep well, night's terrors spurning;
Thou'lt see the sun returning.

Thy word performed, now waking,
I see the bright dawn breaking,
Safe kept from ills unnumbered
While 'neath Thy care I slumbered.

An off'ring Thou desirest.
Behold what Thou requirest.
Nor lamb nor incense bringing,
I come with prayer and singing.

Nor wilt Thou now despise them,
But in Thy heart wilt prize them,
Well knowing, yea, and surely
My best I offer purely.

Approve my works when shown Thee.
Help Thou good councils only;
Beginning, middle, closing,
Lord, for the best disposing.

With blessings guard me waking,
My heart Thy dwelling making,
And with Thy Word, Lord, feed me
Whilst heavenward Thou dost lead me.

Paul Gerhardt, 1648, Tr. A. Ramsey, 1916.

Prayer for Tuesday Evening.

Lord, Merciful God, Holy Father, in the daytime do I cry unto Thee with my voice, in my distress I call upon Thee, and at eventime I remember Thy goodness and mercy, which Thou hast wrought for me. And especially do I magnify Thee now, that purely out of fatherly grace and mercy, without any merit or worthiness on my part, Thou hast this day preserved me from all harm and danger and kept me from sudden death. Therefore do I now and at all times render unto Thee praise and thanksgiving, and pray Thee, for the sake of the bitter sufferings of Jesus Christ, to forgive me wherever I have sinned against Thee this day. Mercifully protect me during the night against my adversary, the devil, and against the fears and terrors of the night. Suffer me to rest without anxieties and worries, and may the eyes of my faith ever behold the lustre of Thy countenance even during the shades of night. For Thou art that shining and true light, which dispels all darkness that surrounds us. Thou, O Lord, art ever with me. Thou art my rock, and my fortress, my deliverer, my strength, in whom I will trust, my buckler, the horn of my salvation, and my high tower.

Lord, my God, at eventime do I lift up my hands unto Thee. Come unto me as the latter rains that make the earth fruitful. Abide with us, for the day is far spent and in the darkness there is none to defend us save Thou alone, our God. Hasten to uphold us. Defend us this night, lest our souls fall into the sleep of sin and our bodies be overcome with evil. Awake us again in due time, and make us to hear joy and peace, for we love Thy word and Thy testimonies, which are the delight of our souls. May our ears be saved from all messages of sorrow, and all anguish be turned from our souls; for Thou canst prosper all that liveth, and fill my life with Thy blessing; in Jesus Christ, our Lord. Amen.

Die Nacht ist kommen, drin wir ruhen sollen.

Now God be with us, for the night is closing;
The light and darkness are of His disposing;
And 'neath His shadow here to rest we yield us,
For He will shield us.

Let evil thoughts and spirits flee before us;
Till morning cometh, watch, O Master, o'er us;
In soul and body Thou from harm defend us,
Thine angels send us.

Let holy thoughts be ours when sleep o'ertakes us;
Our earliest thoughts be Thine when morning wakes us;
All day serve Thee, in all that we are doing
Thy praise pursuing.

As Thy beloved, soothe the sick and weeping,
And bid the prisoner lose his griefs in sleeping;
Widows and orphans, we to Thee commend them;
Do Thou befriend them.

We have no refuge, none on earth to aid us,
Save Thee, O Father, Who Thine own hast made us;
But Thy dear presence will not leave them lonely,
Who seek Thee only.

Father, Thy name be praised, Thy kingdom given;
Thy will be done on earth as 'tis in heaven;
Keep us in life, forgive our sins, deliver
Us now and ever.

Petrus Herbert, 1566., St. 5, Anon., 1627, Tr. Catherine Winkworth, 1863.

Prayer for Wednesday Morning.

Almighty, All-gracious God! All Thy creatures should praise and glorify Thee. The birds under the heavens magnify Thee with lovely songs early in the morning as their Lord and Maker. So will I too heartily thank Thee, that Thou hast preserved me under Thy shelter and protection during the night now past, and all my life even to the present hour, and awakening me from the sleep of the darkness of this night, hast suffered me to arise again in health and joy. I pray Thee for the sake of the saving resurrection of Jesus Christ from the dead, that Thou wouldst ever keep me together with all my loved ones from all danger and evil.

O Lord, save Thy people, and bless Thine inheritance: feed them also, and lift them up for ever. Fill me also at this early hour with Thy grace, that I may pass this day rejoicing in Thy commandments, and free from mortal sin. Let me experience Thy grace as a dew from the womb of the morning, and as the refreshing moisture that diffuses at the break of day, making the land fruitful. Thou wouldest spread Thy goodness over me, that I may gladly and zealously do Thy will. Govern me with Thy Holy Spirit that I may serve Thee in righteousness and holiness of truth, well pleasing in Thy sight. Guard me that I sin not against Thee, nor defile my conscience with carnal lusts that militate against the soul. Keep my tongue from evil, and my lips from speaking guile. Foolish talking or jesting, unbecoming of Christians, be ever far removed from me. Grant, that I offend none with my lips, nor backbite, judge nor condemn, defame nor vilify. O that I might put a lock to my lips and seal them with a strong seal, that they bring me not to naught, nor my tongue destroy me.

Give me grace that I may know my shortcomings and correct them, and not fall into Thy righteous judgment and condemnation. Grant my prayer, O Eternal God, for the sake of Thy dear Son, Jesus Christ. Amen.

Morgenglanz der Ewigkeit.

Dayspring of Eternity,
Light from endless Light proceeding,
Let Thy beams upon us shine
As the shadows are receding;
And dispel by Thy great might
Our dark night.

As the soft refreshing dew
Falls upon the drooping flower,
So our fainting hearts renew
By Thy Spirit's quickening power;
Ne'er Thy bounteous grace withhold
From Thy fold.

Let the glow of Thy pure love
All our icy coldness banish;
In the radiance from above
May our doubts and fears all vanish,
That ere dying we may be
Found in Thee.

O Thou glorious Sun of grace,
May Thy light be ne'er denied us!
Till we reach the heavenly place
Shine upon our way to guide us,
That at last among the blest
We may rest.

Christian Knorr v. Rosenroth, 1684, Tr. J. F. Ohl, 1915.

Prayer for Wednesday Evening.

Most Holy Trinity, One in essence, Three in person, who art my life, salvation, and eternal joy, I praise and thank Thee with mouth and heart that Thou hast so graciously protected me throughout this day. I pray Thy divine goodness to cover up all my shortcomings, and especially where this day, with my tongue, with vain and unprofitable words, slander or otherwise, I have sinned against Thee and Thy holy commandments. According to Thy name, O God, so is Thy praise unto the ends of the earth: Thy right hand is full of righteousness.

Therefore I commend my body and my soul into Thy hands. Thy divine Majesty bless me; Thy holy Trinity shelter me; Thy eternal Unity preserve me. May Thy unbounded mercy protect me; Thy inexpressible benevolence defend me, the sublime truth of God cover me; profound knowledge of Christ strengthen me; the unfathomable goodness of the Lord keep me. The grace of the Father govern me; the wisdom of the Son refresh me; the power of the Holy Spirit enlighten me. My Creator aid me, my Redeemer quicken me, my Comforter abide with me. The Lord bless me and keep me. The Lord make His face shine upon me and be gracious unto me. The Lord lift up His countenance upon me and give me peace. The protection and blessing of the one and eternal Godhead be between me and all mine enemies, visible and invisible, today and always, that they may not approach nor injure me. As the pillar of the cloud went between the army of the Egyptians and the army of Israel, so that they could not come together, and no harm befall the children of Israel, so mayest Thou be a pillar of fire and a wall of separation between me and mine enemies, that no harm come over me.

Keep me also in my last hour. When mine eyes no longer see, mine ears no longer hear, my tongue no longer speak, be Thou with me, O blessed Trinity, that the Evil One have no power over me. Amen.

Hirte deiner Schafe.

Shepherd never sleeping, In Thy gracious keeping
I have been today.
Thou art my Defender, So in mercy tender
Come and with me stay;
All this night Keep me in sight,
Send Thine angels to attend me
And protection lend me.

While I lie and slumber, Let Thine hosts outnumber
All my raging foes.
Be of grace the Giver, And Thy child deliver
From guilt's painful throes.
For Thy Son My soul hath won;
By His wounds, so sorely stricken,
He my heart doth quicken.

Shield Thou from all danger Ev'ry lonely stranger
And my dear ones, too.
Tenderly embrace us And with mercy grace us,
Be our Father true.
Thou with me And I with Thee,
Thus shall I, mine eyelids closing,
Be in peace reposing.

Close the door behind us, Let no evil find us,
Keep all ills away.
Be our shield and cover, Let Thine angels hover
O'er us now, we pray.
By sweet rest Let us be blest,
Ev'ry fear of Satan's raging
In our hearts assuaging.

What if death should take me And no light awake me
From my sleep and rest?
If Thou hast intended That my life be ended,
Let Thy name be blest;
As for me, I yield to Thee.
In the wounds of Jesus lying,
I am daily dying.

By no cares encumbered, Though my hours be numbered,
I now fall asleep.
All to Thee commending Who Thine hosts are sending
Watch o'er me to keep.
Through the night Be my delight,
And if I should see the morrow,
Thou wilt cure all sorrow.

Benjamin Schmolcke, 1715, Tr. H. Brueckner, 1918.

41

Prayer for Thursday Morning.

Jesus Christ, Thou art the eternal light, which dispelleth the darkness of night and the shadow of death: I magnify Thy name, I glorify and thank Thee. For Thou hast so graciously kept me during this night, and hast brought me out of the darkness to the light of day. Thou hast shielded me against the terrors of the night, the snares of the devil, the noisome pestilence, that walketh in the darkness, manifold illness and disease. Thou hast guarded and watched over my soul, even as the shepherd watches over his flock. And all that I possess is kept from harm through Thy great mercy.

Praise and thanks be said unto Thee for Thy gracious protection and all Thy gifts. I will speak of Thy power and magnify Thy goodness, when the day breaks. For Thou art my refuge, my strong tower, my present help, my faithful God, in whom I trust. Thou makest glad my heart and my countenance rejoiceth. I pray Thee, for the sake of Thy holy birth and incarnation, suffer Thy grace to rise in my heart and break forth even as the beauty of the morning, and come over me as the early rain. Illumine me with Thy radiance, and be Thou the light of my heart, for Thou art the right day star and the true light, that lighteth men to the eternal life.

Be merciful unto me, O Lord, for in Thee do I put my trust. My soul waiteth for Thee, more than they that watch for the morning, yea more than they that watch for the morning. Be Thou mine arm in the morning, my salvation also in the time of trouble. Protect me in body and soul, that no evil befall me and no plague come nigh unto my dwelling. Keep from me all wicked spirits. Defend me from evildoers. Stand up for me against the workers of iniquity and shield me, that the hands of mine adversaries may not touch me.

O Lord, our God, establish Thou the work of our hands upon us; yea, the work of our hands establish Thou it, and strengthen our hands, and teach us that we may keep Thy commandments and sin not against Thee this day. Grant us this for the sake of Thy mercy, which endureth for ever and ever. Amen.

Wach auf, mein Herz, die Nacht ist hin.

Awake, my soul; the rising sun
Dispels the night of mourning;
Awake, with songs of praises run
To greet the Lord returning.
He burst the gates of death today
And left the gloomy grave for aye
While all the world rejoices.

Arise, my soul, from sin and death,
To thee new life is given;
Arise and run the race of faith;
Fix thy desires on heaven
Where Jesus, thy Redeemer reigns,
And seek the things that it contains,
If thou with Him be risen.

Art thou distressed by weight of care?
Thy Saviour will remove it.
Believing, thou with joy canst bear
Thy cross and learn to love it.
Cast all thy burden on the Lord;
Fear not; for He will help afford,
For now He hath arisen.

Now Judah's Lion, true and tried,
The victory obtaineth;
The Lamb of God, the Crucified,
For us salvation gaineth,
And giveth righteousness and life;
For after all the dreadful strife,
O'er every foe He triumphs.

Then up, my soul, begin the fight,
For Christ, the Victor, leadeth.
He arms thee with a victor's might;
With Him thy cause succeedeth.
Now thou can'st rise and live anew
And righteousness and peace pursue
And be a faithful servant.

Fear not the angry jaws of hell,
Nor world, nor death, nor devil.
Thy Saviour lives and all is well,
Though sore has been His travail.
A Victor crowned, He as a Friend
The mean and feeble doth attend,
And therefore thou shalt conquer.

Ah, Lord, whom death could not defile,
Who from the dead hast risen,
Free us from Satan's might and guile
And save us from his prison.
O grant, that, as one body, we
May enter that new life in Thee
Which Thou for us hast gotten.

Laurentius Laurenti, 1700, Tr. A. Ramsey.

Give ear to my words, O Lord; consider my meditation. Hearken unto the voice of my cry, my King and my God: for unto thee will I pray.—Ps. v. 1. 2.

Prayer for Thursday Evening.

Praise be to Thee, O God, our Father, through Jesus Christ in the Holy Ghost, one, eternal God, who through Thy manifold compassion hast kept me this day, a poor sinner and miserable creature, from the fiery darts of Satan that fly by day, from the destruction that wasteth at noonday, and hast graciously protected me from a sudden and evil death. Thy mercy, O Lord, is in the heavens; and Thy faithfulness reacheth unto the clouds. Thou art gracious and merciful, and all Thine acts are glorious. I pray Thee, O merciful God, graciously to forgive me all that I have done against Thee this day, in thought, word, or deed. Turn Thy mercy toward me, that I may slumber and rest during this coming night, and that I may never turn from Thee, who art the eternal rest.

Suffer me ever to abide in Thee in the true faith, and safely to sojourn under Thy protection, so that the enemy may never come nigh unto me, nor do me injury. Lord, Thou art my light and my salvation; whom shall I fear? Thou art the strength of my life; of whom shall I be afraid? My heart trusteth in Thee, and I am helped. Thou art my strength and my great shield. Thy right hand strengtheneth me. Thy right hand gladdeneth my heart, and in the shadow of Thy wings will I make my refuge. Behold, my God, in the daytime do I cry unto Thee, and Thou hearest me, and in the night season I am not silent, and Thou answereth my prayer. I remember Thee on my bed, and meditate on Thee in the night watches, because Thou hast been my help. Therefore in the shadow of Thy wings will I rejoice. My soul cleaves unto Thee, for Thy right hand defends me. When darkness comes over me, then Thou, O Lord, art my light and my salvation. O gracious God, vouchsafe unto me Thy grace, so that when that last hour cometh, and I lay me down on my deathbed for the eternal rest, through Thy help, in the true faith, in all confidence and trust, I may happily fall asleep for the eternal life.

Meanwhile keep me in Thee, that I may ever watch and pass my days in all sobriety and moderation, and be found in Christian readiness, since I can not know the hour when Thou comest, O God, to call me hence, so that I may be worthy to stand before the Son of Man, and be not put to shame; who liveth and reigneth with Thee and the Holy Ghost, world without end. Amen.

Nur in Jesu Blut und Wunden.

Now in Jesus' wounds reposing,
I my tired eyes am closing.
For His love and pardoning grace
Are my only resting place.

Through the day His mercy holds me,
And by night His arm enfolds me.
Of Thy strong protection sure,
Jesus, I shall rest secure.

Tr. H. Brueckner, 1916.

Prayer for Friday Morning.

Blessed be God, my Maker! Blessed be God, my Saviour! Blessed be God, my Comforter! Who giveth unto me my health, my life, and every blessing; my very present help and my protection. Thou hast kept me according to Thy great and most blessed compassion during this night now past against the onslaughts of Satan, and preserved me in health. I beseech Thee, Heavenly Father, through Jesus Christ, Thy dear Son, take me this day also into Thy divine protection, and shield me that no evil may assail my life.

For into Thy hands do I this day and all days commend my body and soul, my thoughts, words, and deeds, all that I do or leave undone, my going out and my coming in, my walks and ways, my rising up and my lying down, my will and counsel, my thoughts and desires, my faith and profession, the end of my life, the day and hour of my death, my passing away and my resurrection. O Lord God, do Thou with me as Thou wilt: for Thou knowest what serves best Thy glory and my salvation. Keep me in Thy fear and in the true knowledge of Thee.

Protect me from the deeds of unrighteousness. And if perchance and by reason of my frailty I sin against Thee, I pray Thee take not from me Thy mercy; turn not from me Thy grace; withdraw not Thy help. For there is none other God nor Helper but Thee, and as there is none before Thee, there is none after Thee. Thou art the first and the last, Alpha and Omega, and there is none other God beside Thee.

Therefore do I call only upon Thee: may Thy goodness rule over me. Cause me to hear Thy loving kindness in the morning; for in Thee do I trust. Lead me on the paths of righteousness, that I may not walk in the counsel of the ungodly, nor stand in the way of sinners, nor yet sit in the seat of the scornful, but that my heart may ever delight in Thy word and commandments, and meditate upon them day and night; through Jesus Christ, our Lord. Amen.

Die helle Sonn leucht jetzt herfuer.

The morning sun shines in the skies,
And we from peaceful slumbers rise.
All praise to God who hath this night
Protected us from Satan's might.

Lord Jesus, shield us now by day
From sin and error on our way.
To us Thy holy angels send,
And let them to our wants attend.

Make Thou our hearts obedient,
To use Thy word and sacrament,
To do Thy will whate'er betide,
Thus pleasing Thee, our trusty guide.

Bless Thou the Labour of our hands
And help us keep Thy law's demands,
That all our work, begun in Thee,
May to Thy praise and glory be.

Nicolaus Hermann, 1560, Tr. H. Brueckner, 1918.

Prayer for Friday Evening.

Blessed be the Lord God, who only doeth wondrous things! And blessed be His glorious name for ever: and let the whole earth be filled with His glory! Daily will I praise the Lord, and at eventime my mouth shall thank Him while I have any being. For when I cry with my voice, He hears me, and gives ear to my supplication. When I pray, He attends to my voice. The Lord is my refuge and strength, a very present help in trouble. Therefore do I laud and magnify Thee, Eternal God, that Thou hast this day so mercifully kept me from every harm and evil.

My heart is glad and my soul glorifies Thee for Thy goodness and mercy. Ever shall my tongue speak of Thee and say, Blessed be the Lord, and blessed be Thy holy name! I pray Thee, graciously pardon, wherever I have this day sinned against Thee, and grant me and mine Thy protection during the coming night. Be Thou my shield, and my shade upon my right hand. O Lord, preserve me from all evil, preserve my soul.

Be gracious unto me, for in Thee do I put my trust. I trust in the Lord, and cry to God, the Highest, to God Who endeth all mine affliction. Behold, He that keepeth Israel shall neither slumber nor sleep. He will guide my steps on the paths of righteousness, that I slip not and my feet do not falter. He will not suffer my feet to be moved, and His word is a light unto my path. Therefore as I lay me down, I will not be afraid of sudden terror, neither of the desolation of wicked people, when it cometh. For Thou keepest my foot from being taken, and deliverest me from the snares of death. O Lord God, lift upon me the light of Thy countenance, that I may lie down and sleep in peace, and dwell in safety under Thy protection. For Thou alone, O Lord, can help me.

In Thy name will I lie down to rest and let my eyelids slumber. Thou, O Lord, wilt again awaken me with rejoicing, to the glory and praise of Thine eternal majesty; through Jesus Christ, our Lord. Amen.

Hinunter ist der Sonnen Schein.

Sunk is the sun's last beam of light,
And now the world is wrapt in night.
Christ, light us with Thy heavenly ray,
Nor let our feet in darkness stray.

Thanks, Lord, that Thou throughout the day
Hast kept all grief and harm away;
That angels tarried round about
Our coming in and going out.

Whate'er of wrong we've done or said,
Let not the charge on us be laid;
That, through Thy free forgiveness blest,
In peaceful slumber we may rest.

Thy guardian angels round us place
All evil from our couch to chase;
Our soul and body, while we sleep,
In safety, gracious Father, keep.

Nicolaus Hermann, 1560, Tr. Frances Elizabeth Cox, 1841.

Prayer for Saturday Morning.

O Thou Very and Eternal God, the Father of our Lord Jesus Christ. To Thee do I lift up my heart in dutiful gratitude. I will not hide Thy righteousness within my heart. I will declare Thy salvation. I will not conceal Thy loving kindness and Thy truth from the great congregation, and all the good that Thou hast shown me will I not keep silent. For it is a good thing to give thanks unto the Lord, and to sing praises unto Thy name, O Most High: to shew forth Thy loving kindness in the morning, and Thy faithfulness every night. Therefore my soul doth magnify Thee, that Thou in Thy immeasurable grace hast kept me during the night now past.

Blessed be Thou, Lord God Sabaoth, who art merciful unto all, that seek Thee and love Thy salvation. Blessed is Thy holy name in all the earth, who art our refuge and our help! Blessed are all Thy works which Thou doest for the children of men! I beseech Thee, protect me this day, that the Evil One may not harm me, and the hands of the wicked touch me not. Lord God, my Saviour, early will I seek Thee, early do I cry unto Thee.

Grant, that I may fulfill the duties of my calling and all that is committed unto me with diligence and trust to the glory of Thy name and the betterment of my fellowman, so that I may not misuse the light of this day, neither any of Thy creatures in the service of sin and vanity, neither grieve Thee, nor transgress the covenant of my Baptism with anything I do or leave undone. Vouchsafe unto me Thy grace, that I may guard myself against the six things which Thou dost hate, yea, seven which are an abomination unto Thee: a proud look, a lying tongue, and hands that shed innocent blood, a heart that deviseth wicked imaginations, feet that are swift in running to mischief, a false witness that speaketh lies, and he that soweth discord among brethren.

From such and the like vices preserve me, O God, that I may nevermore be led nor consent to them, but teach me to do Thy will; for Thou art my God: Thy Spirit is good. Lead me into the land of uprightness, that I may serve Thee in a life that is without blame, and my deeds and all my conduct be pleasing in Thy sight; for Christ's sake. Amen.

Die gueldne Sonne.

The sun, ascending, To us is lending
Bliss, joy, and gladness, Cure for all sadness,
Filling the world with its rich, golden light.
I was reclining When no light was shining;
But the sun's beauty Now calls me to duty,
As I behold it so fair and so bright.

Mine eye beholdeth What God unfoldeth:
Heaven's bright glory Tells me the story
Of His unlimited power and love,
And how the sainted In beauty untainted,
Free from things mortal, Beyond death's dark portal,
Dwell in the heavenly mansions above.

To God in heaven Be praises given;
Come, let us offer And gladly proffer
To the Creator the gifts that we prize.
He well receiveth A heart that believeth,
Hymns that adore Him Are precious before Him
And to His throne like sweet incense arise.

At the day's ending Sweet slumbers sending,
And in the morning All things adorning,
These are His works and His blessings so true.
When night descendeth Protection He lendeth
When morn appeareth Our spirits He cheereth,
Causing His mercy to crown us anew.

Father above me, Thou who dost love me,
Bless my beginning, Keep me from sinning,
Move ev'ry hindrance well out of my way.
Strength ever lend me, From Satan defend me,
Spare me temptation, So that in my station
I may Thy holy commandments obey.

Let me with pleasure See the full measure
Which upon others, Who are my brothers,
Thou of Thy blessings dost richly bestow.
Bid envy vanish! All greediness banish!
Make me Thy dwelling, Sin's darkness dispelling.
Grant that in virtue I daily may grow.

What is man's being? It is like seeing
Autumn's bleak shadows Sweep o'er the meadows
When the cold winds drive the clouds on their way.
All that we cherish Must crumble and perish.
Plants must stop growing, And stars must cease glowing;
Heaven and earth are not destined to stay.

All else decayeth, God only stayeth,
He of creation Is the foundation.
His will and word must forever abide.
His grace endureth And for us secureth
Comfort in sorrow And help for the morrow,
Keeping us cheerful, whate'er may betide.

God of creation, Be my salvation!
Calm all my terrors, Blot out my errors,
Grant that Thy pardon I fully may share;
Withal attend me, Rule, guide, and defend me
In mercy tender, Because I surrender
Soul, will, and all to Thy fatherly care.

Whilst Thou art giving What for a living
Seems very needful, Oh, make Thou me heedful
Of this great truth and commendable thought:
God, like a tower, Transcends all in power;
Good beyond telling, In beauty excelling,
He doth suffice me, all else counts for naught.

If grief and sadness Temper my gladness
If for the morrow Thou send me sorrow
Do as Thou wilt, for my trust is in Thee.
Thou surely knowest That what Thou bestowest,
E'en though distressing, Must bring me a blessing;
Thou wilt not deal too severely with me.

Ills that still grieve me Soon are to leave me;
Though waves may tower And winds gain power,
After the storm the fair sun shows its face.
Joys e'er increasing, And peace never ceasing,
These I shall treasure And share in full measure
When in His mansions God grants me a place.

Paul Gerhardt, 1666, Tr. H. Brueckner, 1918.

Prayer for Saturday Evening.

Praise be unto Thee, Thou great and unchangeable God! Praise be unto Thy goodness and mercy! Praise be unto Thy eternal wisdom and truth, that Thou hast preserved me during the day now past from all danger and harm. I pray Thee, graciously perfect Thy goodness which Thou hast begun in me, and suffer me to rest this night under Thy protecting shield, and cover me with Thy wings.

Suffer me to put my trust under the shadow of Thy hands, that I fear no evil. Keep me, O God, as the apple of the eye. Hide me under the shadow of Thy wings. Lord, Thou art the portion of mine inheritance; my salvation is in Thy hands. Grant unto me, according to Thy goodness, that neither fear nor trembling come over me, and no terrors of the night overwhelm me. Be merciful unto me, for in Thee do I put my trust, and under the shadow of Thy wings do I find my refuge. I seek the Lord in the time of need; my hand is outstretched in the night without ceasing; for my soul has none other comfort; and I know of none other helper in heaven or earth but Thee alone.

At midnight when I awaken, I meditate upon Thy name, so altogether lovely, upon Thy goodness and fidelity, vouchsafed unto me, and I praise Thee because]of Thy righteous judgments. When I am troubled I remember God, when my spirit is overwhelmed I speak of my Saviour. For He redeemeth my life from destruction and saveth me from the snares of death. Lord God, my Saviour, by day and by night do I cry unto Thee, pardon all my transgressions, which during this day and the week now past I have committed against Thee.

O Lord, deliver my soul for Thy mercy's sake. Thou art gracious and just, and our God is merciful. The Lord preserveth the simple. I was brought low, and He helped me. Therefore will I rejoice and praise Thee, and sing aloud upon my bed. For the days of my life will appear as noonday, and darkness as the morning's light, and I will rejoice that Thou, O God, art my hope and my rest in life and death.

I lay me down, and none will terrify me. Thus do I commend my body and soul into Thy hands, Thou Faithful God. Thou hast redeemed me through Jesus Christ, our Lord. Amen.

Werde munter, mein Gemuete.

Soul of mine, to God awaking,
And ye senses, ev'ry one,
Come, your quiet haunts forsaking,
Tell what God to me has done.
How He this entire day
Has been with me on my way,
To my many wants attending
And from ills protection lending.

Praise and thanks to Thee I render,
Father Thou of mercies great.
Thou hast been my strong Defender,
And Thy love does not abate.
Thou hast shielded me from woe,
Lent me strength and quenched the foe,
So that I, such help beholding,
Rest secure in Thine enfolding.

If from Thee I have departed,
I return again to Thee,
Knowing Thou art tender-hearted,
Since Thy Son has died for me.
I can not deny the guilt,
But for me His blood was spilt,
And Thy grace, all sin exceeding,
Lends forgiveness at His pleading.

O Thou Light, with brightness filling
Ev'ry true and pious soul,
Into me Thy grace instilling,
Make my troubled spirit whole.
Deign this night to stay with me,
And let me abide in Thee,
That, while darkness may enthrall me,
Yet no evil may befall me.

Grant that I in peace may slumber,
Finding sweet and quiet rest.
Let no cares my soul encumber,
Keep it by Thy presence blest.
Mind and body, child and wife,
All my goods and all my life,
Friends and foes (again befriended)
Be this night to Thee commended.

Let no terrors overtake me,
Shield me well from base attack.
Let no grievous pain awake me,
War and pestilence keep back.
Ward off fire, water, death,
All that threatens life and breath.
Spare me violence, extortion
And, withal, a sinner's portion.

O immortal God, endue me
With the gifts for which I ask.
Jesus, lest some ill pursue me,
Prosper me in ev'ry task.
Holy Spirit, comfort, friend,
On whose counsel I depend,
Listen to my earnest pleading,
Amen. Thou my prayer art heeding.

Johann Rist, 1642, H. Brueckner, 1918.

Personal Prayers

A Daily Prayer, to be spoken mornings or evenings. Dear God and Lord! I live, yet know not how long. I die, yet know not when. Thou, O Heavenly Father, knowest. Lo, dear Lord, is this hour, this day (this night) the last of my life: Thy will be done! Thou alone knowest best. As Thou wilt I am willing through the true faith in Jesus Christ, my Redeemer, to live or die. But, O God, do Thou grant me this petition, that I may not suddenly pass away in my sins, and be lost. Vouchsafe unto me true knowledge, repentance and sorrow over my passed transgressions. Set them before my sight in this life, that they may not at the last day be set before me, and I be put to shame before angels and men.

Grant me sufficient time and opportunity for repentance, so that from all my heart I may know and acknowledge my transgressions, and from Thy saving word obtain forgiveness and comfort for the same. O Merciful Father, forsake me not, and take not Thy Holy Spirit from me. My heart and my heart's trust, O Thou Searcher of hearts, is ever known to Thee. Keep me in such trust to the life eternal. May I die, when Thou wilt, only grant me a peaceful and blessed End. Amen.

At the Beginning of the Week's Work. Rule Thou, O God the Father, who hast made us, and like all other creatures ordained us not to indolence but to work, and bless each one in his calling. Thou who rulest the universe also rule our own dear government and graciously vouchsafe to it Thy wisdom and strength.

Rule Thou, O God the Son, who hast redeemed and ransomed us from sin. Take from us the burden of sin committed during the week now past, and graciously grant us Thy peace. Thou the Supreme Bishop and Archshepherd of our souls, help all servants of Thy word in this and all Thy congregations on earth to Labour and bring forth much fruit unto eternal life.

Rule Thou, O God the Holy Ghost, who hast sanctified us and born us again in Holy Baptism. Create in us a clean heart and renew a right spirit within us, that we carry no evils of the past into the new week, but put away all purpose and inclination of the old Adam still in us. Govern Thou our hearts with power; and if this week mark for any of us the end of life, help Thou in the last bitter hour. Fill the heart with that grace which is better than life. Teach the hands to battle and vanquish the last enemy, and grant for Christ's sake, the rest and triumph of the sabbath everlasting.

Thou, the Triune and Immortal God, be and abide with us and Thy Church forever. Unto Thee be glory, laud, and honor, world without end. Amen.

Prayer for a Pious Life. O my dear Lord Jesus, illumine me today and evermore, that I may shape the course of my Christian life and direct it toward the eternal Jerusalem, my eternal home. And as Thou yearnest for me, may I also have all my delight and thirst in Thee, seek Thee early, yearn for Thee, and make of Thee, the bread of life, the companion of all my ways.

Keep me, O unchangeable, everlasting God, from the inconstancy of the children of this world, that I may not fall into hypocrisy as they do, but today and always, in all my calling, prove myself constant in godliness, so that my life may decrease in vice and increase in virtue. May I always faithfully serve Thee, my Lord, disdain the worldly, be exalted in Thee, experience Thy grace and protection, and eternally thank Thee, for Christ's sake. Amen.

Prayer for Sincere Repentance. Merciful and Gracious God, Thou art slow to anger and plenteous in mercy! Thou callest us daily through the gracious preaching of Thy word to devout conversion, and in Thy name causest repentance and remission of sins to be preached. And Thou showest Thy forbearance with us through Thy long suffering and inexpressible mercy, and dost not suddenly come upon sinners in the midst of their evil deeds with Thy righteous wrath and judgment to punish them, but giveth place and time for repentance, so that no one can justly charge or accuse Thee. For Thou art not willing that any should perish, but that all should come to repentance and have everlasting life. O dear God, Thou knowest the sluggishness of our flesh and the hardness of our hearts, that we through inherited sin are thus far deranged and so deeply sunk in sin, that of our own accord we can not rise or return. Therefore, for the sake of the wounds of Jesus Christ, my Lord, I beseech Thee, convert Thou me, and I am converted. For Thou art my God, and where I am converted I will truly repent. Save Thou me, O Lord, and I am saved. Help me, and I am helped. Behold, I am like an erring and lost sheep. Seek Thou Thy servant, that I forget not Thy commandments. Circumcise the foreskin of my heart. Purge me, and I shall be clean. Wash me, and I shall be whiter than snow. Create in me a clean heart, O God; and renew a right spirit within me.

Cast me not away from Thy presence; and take not Thy Holy Spirit from me. O dear God, look upon me, as Thou didst look upon Mary Magdalene, the repentant sinner, as she lay at Thy feet and wept over her transgressions; and the publican in the temple, as he smote his breast and besought Thy grace.

Vouchsafe unto me sincere sorrow and contrition over my sin, and a true faith with firm confidence in Thy grace, and also worthy fruits of repentance. Let me discern the day of Thy visitation, and not despise the riches of Thy mercy, so that I may not neglect the accepted time, and the day of Thy salvation, and not fail to turn to Thee, my Lord and God. May I not postpone my repentance from one day to another, nor yet to the last hour, but rather turn to Thee this day and repent. Amen.

Prayer for the Forgiveness of Sins. Merciful Father, Eternal God, my sins are grievous, many and great my transgressions, and mine iniquities are innumerable, for the imaginations of my heart are evil from my youth. O Lord, who can understand his errors? Behold, I acknowledge my transgressions: my sin is ever before me. Against Thee only have I sinned, and done evil in Thy sight: that Thou mightest be justified when Thou speakest, and be clear when Thou judgest. I beseech Thine infinite mercy, enter not into judgment with Thy servant: for in Thy sight shall no living man be justified. If Thou, Lord, shouldest mark iniquities, O Lord, who shall stand? Behold, if Thou contendest with man, he can not answer Thee one of a thousand, for all our righteousness before Thee is as the filthy rag. Have mercy upon me, O God, according to Thy loving kindness: according to the multitude of Thy tender mercies, blot out my transgressions. Wash me thoroughly from mine iniquity, and cleanse me from my sin for Thy name's sake. Lord, have mercy upon me, save my soul, for, alas! I have sinned against Thee.

Remember, O Lord, Thy tender mercies and Thy loving kindnesses; for they have been ever as of old. Remember not the sins of my youth, nor my transgressions: according to Thy mercy remember Thou me for Thy goodness' sake, O Lord. Remember that we are flesh, as the wind which bloweth and doth not return, and cease in Thy anger and wrath against us. O merciful God, I acknowledge that my virtues and my deeds can never blot out my sins, nor yet merit Thy grace. Only the innocent suffering and death of Jesus Christ, the Lamb without spot or blemish, is the true offering for our iniquities, and His blood, shed for the remission of our sins, is the cleansing and purification of our souls. In such confidence and hope I supplicate Thee: forgive Thou the transgressions of Thy people. Cover our sins. Impute not our iniquities, for Thou art merciful. Cleanse Thou me from secret fault. Let my sorrowing soul and my vexed bones again rejoice, for with Thee there is mercy and plenteous redemption. O Lord, hear the voice of my supplication, and despise not the groanings of my heart, for Christ's sake. Amen.

Prayer for True Faith. Lord, Almighty God, Thou Father of lights, with whom there is no variableness, neither shadow of turning, from whom every good and perfect gift cometh, I pray Thee, since all men have not faith: implant and maintain in my heart through the workings of Thy Holy Spirit the true knowledge of Thy dear Son Jesus Christ, and increase it from day to day, so that I, too, may be filled with the knowledge of Thy will in all wisdom and spiritual understanding, that I may walk worthy of Thee unto all pleasing, being faithful in every good work, and increase in such knowledge according to Thy glorious power in all patience and long suffering with joy. Grant unto me, according to the riches of Thy glory, that I may be strengthened with might by Thy Spirit in the inner man, that Christ may dwell in my heart by faith. O dear God, since no man knoweth the Son but Thou, O Father, and no man knoweth Thee, the Father, but only the same Thy Son, and he to whom the Son will reveal Thee, I pray Thee, draw Thou me unto Thee. Grant me the knowledge of salvation, which is the forgiveness of sins. Strengthen my weak faith, which is small as the mustard seed, so that it may increase, and I be rooted and grounded in Thee, and may stand steadfast and unmoveable. Gracious God, Thou hast kindled the spark of faith in my heart and has begun this good work in me, I cry to Thee, perfect it until the end, that we may ever increase in knowledge and understanding, and be sincere and without offense till the day of Christ, being filled with the fruits of righteousness, which are by Jesus Christ, unto the glory and praise of God. Preserve what Thou hast begun, that we might war a good warfare, holding faith and a good conscience, and not waver or succumb in trial and temptation and make shipwreck concerning faith. Therefore protect me, my God, that I am not led astray among the errors, schisms, and heresies of the world. Preserve me from superstitions and all false doctrine, that I may neither err nor doubt in any article of faith. And vouchsafe unto me Thy grace, that my faith be not lifeless, inactive, or without good fruits, but active and energetic, serving in love, so that I, too, may carry off the end of faith, which is the soul's salvation. Amen.

Prayer on the Eve of a Journey. Almighty and Gracious God and Father, Thou protector of all that trust in Thee from their hearts! In Thy name will I proceed and undertake this journey. For Thou art my God and preservest my going out and my coming in. Thou leadest my feet in right paths and wilt not suffer them to be moved. I heartily beseech Thee to be my gracious guide and companion on this present journey. Send Thy holy angels, and command them, in all my wanderings, to keep me from all evil in body and soul. Lead me on the paths of the righteous and bring me safely to my destination, that I may laud and magnify Thee, here in time and in eternity forever. And now, O Lord God and Father, into Thy hands do I commit my body and soul and all that I possess. Thy holy angel be my safe guard. Amen.

Prayer During a Journey. Almighty and Most Merciful God! We are always in Thy sight wherever we be. Thou preservest our coming in and our going out, and leadest us on the right paths that we slip not. I pray Thee, that as Thou didst lead Thy servant Abraham from the land of the Chaldees and kept him unharmed in his pilgrimage, and didst say to his grandson Jacob when he journeyed to Mesopotamia, I am with thee, and will bring thee again into this land; and as Thou also didst lead the Children of Israel through the Red Sea and through the desert, and didst go before them, by day in a pillar of a cloud and night in a pillar of fire: thus wouldst Thou also be with me on my wandering, protect me on land and sea, by day and by night, and keep me from all harm and danger. And when my business is completed bring me home again in full health of body and soul. And as Thou didst accompany youthful Tobias through Thy angel Raphael, likewise do Thou accompany me in all my ways, so that when I, too, have happily returned to my home, I with all mine own may have the greater reason to laud and praise Thee as my true and faithful guide. Meanwhile I commend to Thy care all that I leave at home, and beseech Thee to have charge concerning them, and suffer me to find them unharmed when I return. Amen.

Thanksgiving After a Completed Journey. Gracious God and Father! Most heartily do I thank Thee that Thou hast enabled me to bring my journey to a happy end. Through the ministrations of Thy dear angels Thou hast again brought me to my home, guarded and kept me from all evil, preserved me from the murderous and robbing hands of evildoers, and the teeth of wild beasts, and kept me from all other dangers of body and soul. In short, that I have been led to and fro in health and happiness: I owe it altogether to Thy fatherly goodness and almighty care. And I beseech Thee from all my heart, continue to keep me and mine under Thy protection, and preserve us, body and soul, to the eternal life, for Jesus' sake. Amen.

A Prayer for School. We pray Thee, everlasting God, Father, Son, and Holy Ghost, Thou eternal and inseparable Trinity and inexpressible Unity, that Thou wouldest faithfully take under Thy protecting wing the flock of Thy Christendom, and ever abide in our midst with Thy grace and truth. Be Thou with us, O Lord, our God. Be Thou a wall of fire round about us, and destroy them who hate Thee and are hostile to Thy name. So rule us, O God, that we may ever be guided by Thy clear and pure word and are not seduced by the external appearance of things. Keep us, Lord Jesus, from error and false doctrine, and send us faithful teachers who take heed unto Thy congregation, purchased with Thy blood, and are anxious to perform Thy will. Grant us obedient hearts, so that we, as lambs of Thy flock, may obey Thy voice, and be filled with fruits of righteousness. Teach us ever to do Thy will, for Thou art our God: Thy spirit is good. Lead us into the land of uprightness, to the end that we, too, through a blessed departure from this life may attain to Thee and the everlasting joy and blessedness, and behold Thy glory to all eternity. Amen.

A Birthday Prayer. Dear Father in heaven, I thank Thee from all my heart, that Thou hast put me into this world and made me a rational being. I am born of Christian parents and made a member of Thy holy Church. Today the anniversary of my birth hath come, and since I have been permitted to reach this day and thus complete another year of my pilgrimage, I thank Thee from all my heart and joyfully reiterate the thanksgiving of Thy servant David, "Bless the Lord, O my soul, and all that is within me bless His holy name. Bless the Lord, O my soul, and forget not all His benefits: who forgiveth all thine iniquities; who healeth all thy diseases; who redeemeth thy life from destruction; who crowneth thee with loving kindness and tender mercies." Since every day of my life, however, is one step nearer to death, which can strike me this hour, yes, this very minute, I beseech Thee so to shape and rule every day of my life, that I may walk according to Thy pleasure as in the day, that is circumspectly in Thy sight, honestly, and conscious of my responsibility, in short as a true Christian and in conformity with the promise made by me to Thee, my dear God, in my baptism. And if this prove my last year and my last birthday, I place all things into Thy gracious keeping. If it is Thy will that I should cease to live, then I have lived enough. For if it is sufficient for Thee, it is sufficient for me. Am I old enough for Thee, I am old enough for me. Here I again put myself under Thy shield and protection, into Thy sublime and eternal power. If I live this year, may I live in Thee; if I die, may I die in Thee, so that I may live, and move, and have my being in Thee, and whether living or dying I may be Thine to all eternity. Amen.

Prayer for Temporal Peace. Eternal God, Everlasting Father! Thou art a God and lover of peace. From Thee all true unity cometh. We pray Thee graciously to protect Thy Christendom on earth against all its enemies, so that we may be kept in peace, and ever serve Thee gladly in faithful doctrine and a pure conduct. Grant us grace, so that all estates and rulers of Christendom may live peacefully and harmoniously in perfect piety and godliness, so that discipline and order prevail, churches and schools be not destroyed, and the country be not devastated nor grievously oppressed. Grant us grace, so that men will content themselves with what they have, and will not for the sake of avarice or lusting after foreign lands and peoples, nor yet because of pride, vain ambitions, and arrogance, enmity, hatred, envy, nor any other cause, incite war, sedition, or revolution in this our country. Hinder all evil counsel and purpose of unstable men, who think only of that which is not good. Put them to naught in their purposes, so that they must retreat and are utterly consumed with terrors. Stretch forth Thine arm to protect us who are named after Thee, so that Thy heritage be not destroyed. Support Thy faithful who rely upon Thee and call upon Thy name. Hear us in our distress, and Thy holy name protect us. Send us help from Thy sanctuary, and strengthen us from on high. Bless the country and the cities in which Thy holy word dwelleth. Prosperity must dwell within their palaces! O merciful God, incline the hearts of all men to a Christian peace and concord, to the which Thou hast called us through Thy word and gospel. And if bitterness prevail among some, help that it be done away with, to the glory of Thy holy name, the spreading of Thy word, and the betterment of Christendom, and that the poor and distressed in the land may rejoice in Thee and praise Thy holy name, for Thou only performest wonders and provest Thy powers among the nations. Amen.

Prayer of a Patient. Lord God, Heavenly Father! Thou art a faithful God, and wilt not suffer any one to be tempted beyond what he is able, but rather with the temptation wilt also make a way to escape, that he may be able to bear it. I supplicate Thee in my great suffering and pain, so shape the cross, that it may not lay too heavily upon me, and strengthen me that I may bear it with patience, and nevermore despair of Thy mercy. O Christ, Thou Son of the living God! Thou hast endured the agony of the cross for me, and hast died for my sins, I beseech Thee with my whole heart, have mercy upon me a poor sinner, and forgive me my transgressions, wherever I have sinned against Thee. Let my faith in no wise diminish. O God Holy Ghost! Thou true comforter in all times of need. Keep me ever in the spirit of patience and supplication. Sanctify me in my reliance upon Thee. Turn not from me in the hour of my death, and lead me from this vale of sorrow to Thyself in heaven. Amen.

Prayer for a Blessed End. O Merciful God, Thou hast put a limit to man's life, which no man can set aside. For he has his definite time, the number of his months rests with Thee. Thou hast numbered all our days, which pass away like a stream, as though we flew away. Man is like grass, which soon withereth, like the flower of the field, which passeth away. Teach me, O merciful God, to know and take to heart, that I, too, must pass away and that my life has a limit, and I must go hence. Behold, my days are as a handbreadth before Thee, and my life as nothing in Thy sight. Every man at his best is altogether vanity. Lord, so teach us to number our days, what it is, that we may apply our hearts unto wisdom. Lord, teach me to remember that I must die, and have no continuing city in this pilgrimage. Make known unto me my short and transient being, that I may often think of my end, so that in this world I may not live unto myself, but live and die unto Thee, so that I may bravely and joyously await the day of my translation and the appearance of Thy dear Son, Jesus Christ, and with a consecrated life and a pious conduct hasten to Him. Bless me, O God, with a blessed departure, and when my hour cometh, that I may joyously die, find a rational end in true knowledge, and that my reason and intellect be not deranged, and I speak no arrogant words or blasphemies against Thee, my Lord, or against my salvation. Preserve me from an evil sudden death and from eternal damnation. Let me not be suddenly overcome by my last hour without warning, but that I may prepare myself with true repentance and sincere faith. And when it comes make me joyous and brave for my temporal death, which only opens the door to the eternal life. May I then, as Thy servant, depart in peace. For mine eyes have seen Thy salvation, which Thou hast prepared before the face of all people; a light to lighten the Gentiles, and the glory of Thy people Israel. Grant that my last word may be that which Thy dear Son spoke on the cross, "Father, into Thy hands do I commend My spirit!" And when I can no longer speak, hear Thou my last sigh through Jesus Christ. Amen.

Church Prayers

Prayer When Going to Church. Almighty God, Heavenly Father, because of Thy great mercy I will go to Thy house and worship Thee in Thy temple in Thy fear. Lord, lead me in the paths of righteousness, and make Thy way straight before my face. Guide me on the paths of Thy commandments, for Thou art my God, and the Lord of my salvation. I delight in Thy sanctuary and rejoice in the congregation of Thy saints, who confess and glorify Thee. How amiable are Thy tabernacles, O Lord of hosts! My soul longeth, yea, even fainteth for the courts of the Lord. O come, let us worship and bow down: let us kneel before the Lord our maker. For He is our God; and we are the people of His pasture, and the sheep of His hand. Magnify the Lord our God, adore at His footstool; for He is holy. I worship Thee, O God, in the accepted time through Thy great mercy. Hear me according to Thy grace. Amen.

A Morning Prayer for Communion Day. Arise, my soul, this is the day which the Lord hath made. We will rejoice and be glad in it. Give thanks unto the gracious and merciful God for His blessings and say: Almighty and Merciful God and Father, I thank Thee from all my heart for the protection of this night, for the refreshing rest, and for the joyous morning, which Thou hast granted unto me. I praise Thee with all my soul for Thy wonderful mercy which blesses me with the forgiveness of my sins. Praised be Thy grace, which is new each morn, and which on this day also bids me to Thy house, and calls and invites me to Thy altar. O Lord, since I, too, would come to Thy Supper with the throngs which celebrate, do Thou Thyself make me ready. As Thou wouldest find a pure residence in me, do Thou cleanse and consecrate my body and soul. Guide me with Thine eye, and lead me with Thy hand to the riches of Thy mercy. Comfort me with Thy countenance, and do not forsake me. As the hart panteth after the water brooks, so panteth my soul after Thee, O God. And, that my sacred resolve may not be hampered, I commend to Thee my body and soul, reason, senses, and thoughts, whatever I do or leave undone, my coming in and going out, my walking, standing, sitting, and resting, my imaginations and aspirations, my faith and confession, and whatever internally or externally I may be or do. O God, preserve in me a devout spirit, and hinder whatever might disturb or hamper me. Receive me into the especial care of Thy grace, and increase in me the work that is now begun. Perfect and complete it according to Thy power and grace to Thy glory and my salvation. Keep me from evil thoughts, from idle imaginations, from all uncleanliness, so that in Thy fear I may begin a consecrated life and continue therein. May the light of my faith shine before men. May I give offense to none, but rather in Christian conduct edify the brethren and direct them to all virtue.

Holy Jesus, do Thou unite with my body and soul on this day. Nourish me with Thy flesh and refresh me with Thy blood, so that my weak faith be strengthened, and receive the assurance of Thy grace, the remission of my sin, and eternal salvation. Invest me with the pure silk of Thy righteousness. Clothe me in the true wedding garment, that I may appear at Thy heavenly board a worthy guest.

Now, Lord God and Father, be my help and my protection! Lord Jesus Christ be my bread, my light, and life! And Thou, O Holy Ghost, illumine and preserve me in the true sanctification, so that in that estate, into which I again am permitted to enter, I may remain for the course of my life. Let me be enveloped in Thee. Without Thee there is only grief. O dear Saviour, let me ever be with Thee. Amen.

Prayer Before Holy Communion. Lord Jesus Christ, Eternal Son of God, I am not worthy to open my lips and receive the most precious sacrament of Thy body and blood. For I am a sin-stained man, but Thou art the Lord whom the heavens can not encompass. How then can a human being who is but dust and ashes be worthy to receive Thy most holy body and precious blood! I well know and acknowledge that my sins are many and that for that reason I am an unworthy guest at Thy table. But I also sincerely believe and confess it with my lips that by Thy grace Thou canst render me worthy. For Thou art omnipotent and gracious. Thou only canst cleanse and make holy whatever took rise in unclean seed. Thou canst transform sinners into true and holy men, when by Thy grace Thou forgivest sin and renewest us with Thy Holy Spirit. Therefore I pray Thee, by Thy power and love grant me grace, that I may worthily approach Thy altar, and not become guilty of Thy body and blood by unworthy eating and drinking, so that I may not receive death in place of life. Grant me grace, that I may know and test myself as a poor sinner, my heart filled with sorrow over mine iniquity, and may properly discern Thy tender and noble body, and Thy holy, precious blood. May my reason, senses, and intellect be ever submissive to Thy word, and may I be earnestly resolved to better and improve my life with Thy help, so that in this precious sacrament, I may not only with my mouth receive Thy body and blood, but also in true faith accept Thee, my Saviour and Redeemer, enthrone Thee in my heart, and find in Thee my life and blessedness. For Thou art the living bread which cometh down from heaven and bringeth life to men. Whoever cometh to Thee shall nevermore hunger, and he that believeth on Thee shall nevermore thirst. Whoever eateth Thy flesh and drinketh Thy blood dwelleth in Thee and Thou in him, and shall never die.

O beloved Lord, my spirit and my mind yearn for Thee. As the hart panteth after the water brooks, so panteth my soul after Thee, O God. My soul thirsteth for God, for the living God: when shall I come and appear before God? Fill me with Thy grace. Amen.

When About to Receive the Sacred Body & Blood of Christ. Lord Jesus Christ, Thy holy body and blood strengthen and preserve me in the true faith unto eternal life. Amen.

Prayer After the Holy Supper. Lord Jesus Christ, with all my heart I thank and glorify Thee, that Thou hast again cleansed me, a poor sinner, from all my sin, and as an earnest of such cleansing and forgiveness of my sin, hast nourished me with Thy body and blood, and like an unclean child, after such purification, hast received me into the fatherly arms of Thy grace and mercy, and put me pure, reproachless, and without blemish before Thy Father. I earnestly pray Thee with all my power, in addition to such blessing, grant me Thy grace through the workings of Thy Holy Ghost, so that I may sufficiently understand such blessing and grace, gratefully accept it, and glorify and praise Thee with all my heart. Grant me strength from above by Thy Holy Spirit, that I may heartily forgive my neighbour wherever he hath sinned against me, even as Thou hast fully and richly forgiven me my great and manifold transgressions, yes, entirely blotted them out and wilt never remember them. Help me to love my neighbour and gladly show him every good, as Thou hast done unto me, and hast shown me more than I can ever sufficiently thank Thee for. Praise and glory be to Thee, O faithful God, together with the Father and the Holy Ghost, world without end. Amen.

Prayer for the Kingdom of God. (Meeting of the Congregation) Gracious and Blessed God, who hast taught, and commanded us above all things and first to seek the kingdom of God and His righteousness: I pray Thee, grant us grace, that Thy holy word may be preached in all the world in all its truth and purity, and we submit our reason to the obedience of faith, and live holy lives according to it as behooves the children of God to Thy pleasing, so that Thy kingdom may come to us, and increase, and many of them, who do not yet believe in the word, be won through a Christian conduct.

Help us, dear God, who are delivered from the power of darkness and are translated into the kingdom of Thy dear Son Jesus Christ, in whom we have redemption through His blood, even the forgiveness of sin, that we may remain in His kingdom, faithfully continue in the wholesome doctrine, and live worthily as children of light in all piety and godliness. And since the kingdom of God cometh not with outward shew, neither consists of mere words, but is power and spirit: grant us grace, that we may be born again from above through Thy saving word and Thy Holy Spirit, co-heirs of life, so that with our hearts we may dwell above where Christ sitteth, and constantly seek the inheritance incorruptible, and undefiled, that fadeth not away. Enable us to be poor in the spirit and humble, and such who sorrow over their sins. Let us be anhungered and athirst, and heartily yearn after righteousness. May we ever be meek, and suffer and overcome whatsoever of persecution and tribulation may assail us, and revilings and undeserved malignings with patience and longsuffering. Keep us from all offenses, whereby Thy holy name is blasphemed and outraged, Thy kingdom hindered and weakened. Grant us grace to practice our faith in works of love and mercy, feeding, clothing, harboring, visiting, comforting the poor and distressed of this world, so that when that great day dawns we may hear the blessed and joyous voice of Thy dear Son: Come ye blessed of My Father, inherit the kingdom prepared for you from the foundation of the world. Amen.

The Little Treasure of Prayers

A translation of the Epitome from the German Larger Treasure of Prayers (Gebets-Schatz) *which features the prayers and devotionals of the Lutheran Church, including some written by the Reformers.*

Morning & Evening Prayers for a Week

Sunday Morning Prayer. Eternal, almighty God and Father! I most heartily praise and thank Thee, that Thou hast graciously, by Thy holy angels, preserved me from all harm and danger both of body and soul, during the past night and all previous time; and I most heartily pray Thee, forgive me all my sins wherewith I have offended Thee, and enlighten my heart with Thy Holy Spirit, that I may daily grow and increase in Thy knowledge. Grant me grace also, that I may, during this day, avoid all sin and shame, and be found in Thy divine will, in order that I may so walk as to be preserved from all evil, may always and constantly keep Thee in my heart and thoughts, and when the time of my departure approaches, grant that I may fall asleep in the true knowledge of Thy dear Son Jesus Christ, unto a blessed and eternal life. Amen.

Sunday Evening Prayer. Lord, almighty God and heavenly Father, I most heartily thank Thee for all Thy goodness and benefits which Thou hast this day so kindly shown unto me, in that Thou hast defended me from evil and preserved my health. And I, Thy dear child, further pray Thee that Thou wouldst mercifully keep me in Thy alone saving word to my last breath, and enlighten my heart with Thy Holy Spirit, that I may know what is good or evil. And wouldst graciously wipe out the remembrance of all the sins which I this day have knowingly done, also of my secret sins, and grant me this night a christian rest, that I may arise again refreshed and in health, to Thy praise. Help also, dear Father, that I may begin a new life, well pleasing in Thy sight, to the salvation of my soul, in Jesus Christ, Thy dear Son, our only Helper. Amen.

Monday Morning Prayer. Holy and faithful God, heavenly Father! I most heartily praise, honor and adore Thee, that during the past night Thou hast permitted me to rest and sleep in safety, and by Thy fatherly love hast awakened me again refreshed and in the enjoyment of health. I most heartily pray Thee that Thou wouldst this day also and always graciously preserve me together with (my dear parents, brothers and sisters, and) all true Christians from all danger and harm both of body and soul, in order that I may always be found in Thy will. For I commend myself, my body and soul, heart, sense, mind and thoughts, all my strivings and aspirations, all I do and all I leave undone, my going in and coming out, my life and death, and everything that I am and can do, to Thy divine protection. May Thy holy angel be and remain with me, that no misfortune may befall me either in body or soul. Grant this for the sake of Jesus Christ, Thy dear Son. Amen.

Monday Evening Prayer. Merciful God, gracious Father! I heartily thank Thee that during the past day and up to the present hour Thou hast graciously protected me from all danger and harm of body and soul, and pray Thee, that, for the sake of Jesus Christ, Thy dear Son, Thou wouldst graciously forgive all the sins which I have this day again committed against Thee in thoughts, words and deeds, and let them be remembered against me no more. And as I am now about to lie down to rest, I pray, Thou wouldst this night also protect and defend me from all harm and danger of body and soul, so that, being defended against the wiles and power of the devil, against evil, harmful and wicked dreams, I may safely rest and sleep this night, and awake again refreshed and in health to Thy honor. I now commend myself entirely into Thy divine hand; Thou hast redeemed me, Thou faithful God. Amen.

Tuesday Morning Prayer. Lord Jesus Christ, Thou only Saviour of the world! to Thee I lift my heart and mind, and thank Thee again, that Thou hast by Thy boundless mercy and love kept me safe and secure this night from the wiles and power of the wicked one. Lord Jesus Christ, Thou art the portion of my inheritance, my salvation is in Thy hands, and besides Thee I know of no Helper in heaven or on earth. Therefore I pray Thee for the sake of Thy unutterable suffering and anguish, of Thy most painful and bitter death, which in great love Thou didst suffer for me, that Thou wouldst be gracious and merciful unto me, and this day and through my whole life bless, spare, preserve and keep me from all sin and evil in this world of sorrow, until Thou shalt take me to eternal joy and blessedness, for Thy most holy name's sake. Amen.

Tuesday Evening Prayer. O eternal and merciful God, God of all riches, who art in heaven, I most heartily thank Thee for Thy great mercy andpaternal providence by which Thou hast again permitted me to end this day in the enjoyment of health. And since I, alas! have not spent this day to Thy praise and honor, and the welfare of my neighbour, inasmuch as my depraved nature is always inclined more to evil than to good, help, Thou faithful God, that I who am conceived and born in sin, may recognize my infirmity and become a partaker of Thy heavenly grace; and teach me to think much and often of my end, that I may prepare myself for it in true repentance, and when it approaches may depart from this world of trouble full of consolation and blessedness, and with all believing Christians be translated into Thy heavenly paradise. In the mean time, as long as I sojourn on earth, take me into Thy almighty protection and mercifully keep and preserve me from all harm and danger of body and soul, for the sake of Jesus Christ, Thy dear Son. Amen.

Wednesday Morning Prayer. O almighty, merciful God, gracious Father in heaven, since Thou hast again kept me safe this night by Thy ministering spirits, the holy angels, and permitted me to see this new day refreshed and in the enjoyment of health, I most heartily give Thee praise, honor and eternal thanks therefore, and pray Thee again, dear heavenly Father, to whose will I subject all that I do and leave undone, my beginning and end, that Thou wouldst henceforth graciously have mercy upon me, and govern all my thoughts and aspirations, my heart, sense, mind and thoughts, all my words and deeds by Thy Holy Spirit, so that I may understand what is good or evil, and that I may this day so walk and live in this evil and perverse world, that I above all things, free from my sins, may have a heartfelt desire for that eternal home which Christ, my Saviour, purchased and secured for me, and may not lose it by reason of my wicked, sinful life. To this end wilt Thou graciously help me with Thy divine love and the power of Thy Holy Spirit, for the sake of Thy dear Son, Jesus Christ. Amen.

Wednesday Evening Prayer. I thank Thee, O almighty God and kind Father, that Thou hast this day again graciously kept me safe from harm both in body and soul. I pray Thee, that Thou wouldst according to Thy great goodness blot out every sin that I have this day committed against Thee and Thy holy commandments with my heart, tongue, or in other ways, and not forsake me, Thy creature, whom Thou hast redeemed with the precious blood of Thy dear Son Jesus Christ, and protect me this night under Thy almighty wings, against the wicked one, who goeth about as a roaring lion, seeking to devour me, so that under the shadow of Thy goodness I may rest and sleep securely, and the wicked one may not be able to approach me or do me any harm. Amen.

Thursday Morning Prayer. God the Father, God the Son, and God the Holy Spirit, Thou ever blessed Trinity! to Thee I resign myself with body and soul both now and forever, and heartily thank Thee that Thou didst not permit the wicked one to harm me during the past night, but didst, by the protection of Thy holy angels, keep me safe to this day. What shall I render unto Thee, wherewith shall I worthily praise Thee? I will give Thee a contrite and broken heart, full of sins like scarlet, but sorrowing and penitent; graciously accept of it, and wash it white as snow in the precious blood of Thy dear Son, my Redeemer, bury it in His holy innocent wounds, and thus do Thou graciously impart to me the forgiveness of all my sins. And help me to hold myself in Christian readiness every day, inasmuch as I do not know, when Thou wilt come, how and where Thou wilt call me hence, so that I may by Thy blessing be conducted to eternal joy. Grant me this, gracious Father, for the sake of Thy dear Son, Jesus Christ. Amen.

Thursday Evening Prayer. Gracious and most merciful God, eternal Father, what heartfelt love and fatherly care Thou hast for me, a poor sinner, in that Thou hast so graciously preserved me all the days and hours of my life, from my earliest youth to the present time, against all the wiles of the devil, and the danger and harm of the wicked world; and I humbly pray Thee, that, according to Thy paternal love toward me, Thou wouldst to all eternity not remember against me what I have done against Thee this day, but mercifully forgive it, and be gracious unto me for the sake of Thy dear Son, Jesus Christ, who became the Surety for all my sins, and keep me and all who are near and dear to me safe this night from sudden death, from danger by fire and water, pestilence and all harm. I therefore commend myself, my body and soul and everything that I have to Thy fatherly protection; may Thy holy angel be with me, that, I may fear no danger. Amen.

Friday Morning Prayer. I, a poor sinner, have now arisen in Thy name, Thou crucified Lord Jesus Christ, who, as the truly patient Lamb for the slaughter, didst suffer for me the most ignominious death on the cross, and with Thy precious blood redeemed me from all my sins, from death, the devil and hell: govern my heart with Thy Holy Spirit, refresh it with the heavenly dew of Thy grace, preserve me with Thy divine love, and hide me this day, both body and soul, in Thy holy wounds; wash me clean from all my sins, keep me in all good works, and lead me from this world of sorrow to eternal joy and glory, Thou most faithful Saviour, Jesus Christ, my only Comfort, Hope and Life. Amen.

Friday Evening Prayer. O Lord Jesus Christ, Thou patient Lamb for the slaughter and holy sacrificial offering for all my sins, and not for mine alone, but for the sins of the whole world! I most heartily thank Thee again that Thou hast so graciously kept both my body and soul under Thy protecting care this day, and pray Thee that Thou wouldst graciously pardon and forgive all my sins which I have committed this day through the weakness of my depraved nature and the enticement of the evil spirit, and which sorely trouble and oppress my heart and conscience; and as I am now about to lie down to rest and sleep, cover me with the wings of Thy grace, and help that I may with my body sleep under them this night in peace and rest, but with my soul may I always watch for Thee, wait for Thy glorious coming to judgment, and with heartfelt longing keep myself in readiness to go with Thee at last to Thy blessed kingdom. Unto this help me, O faithful God! blessed forevermore with Thy dear Son and the Holy Spirit. Amen.

Saturday Morning Prayer. O thou faithful Father in heaven! Could I but sufficiently praise and thank Thee for all the benefits Thou hast bestowed upon me during all the days of my life! But this is beyond my power and ability. For I am flesh and blood, which can do nothing but what is evil. But Thou doest daily grant me blessings without number, and especially in the past night, if Thou hadst not been my Shield and Defence, the devil would have injured me greatly with his power, so that I could not have arisen in health. But by Thy gracious protection I have been kept safe. I humbly pray Thee, extend to me Thy grace this day, and mercifully keep me, who am Thine through the blood of Christ, henceforth unto eternal life. Amen, Lord Jesus, take my soul into Thy hands and let me be commended unto Thee. Amen.

Saturday Evening Prayer. Merciful, gracious God and Father! Most heartily do I again give Thee praise and thanks, that Thou hast during the whole period of my life taken thought for me in such a fatherly manner, and hast so graciously protected me from all harm and danger of soul and body during this day, even during the whole week up to the present hour. And I further pray Thee, that Thou wouldst through Thy grace, which all penitent sinners have with Thee, blot out all my sins, which I have this day and through the whole week committed knowingly or unknowingly against Thee and my neighbour, and let them be remembered against me no more for ever. And help me graciously that I may pass from the old week into a new Christian life, well-pleasing to Thee, and to all the elect in heaven. May I be commended to Thy gracious arms this night, that I may rest and sleep safely, and arise again refreshed and in health further to praise Thee. And when my last hour comes, take me to Thee, Lord Jesus Christ; for I am Thine and Thou art mine, how gladly and willingly would I soon be with Thee! Amen.

Personal Prayers

Complaint of a poor Sinner concerning the Impenitence of his Heart. I, miserable afflicted sinner, come unto Thee, my heavenly Father, and bring nothing with me but sin only. I can therefore not lift up my eyes to Thy exalted and most holy majesty, but I am ashamed, that I have so oft offended Thee and not hearkened unto Thy voice. Alas! there is nothing good in me, I am conceived and born in sins, my nature is so perverted and depraved, that I cannot feel and experience in me either a desire or love for virtue and the heavenly gifts, but only for transitory honor and joys and the inclination to all evil. I have lived in sin from my youth up, and yet I live in sin, as long as I have this sinful flesh of Adam on me. But, dear Lord, I comfort myself by Thy unbounded, unfathomable, infinite and unspeakable grace and mercy, which Thou hast promised to all penitent sinners in Thy word and confirmed by a sacred oath. I comfort myself by the precious merit of Thy only begotten Son, who was delivered for the sake of my sins and raised for my justification. O heavenly Father, hide Thy face from my sins and behold the face of Thy Son, who in himself never did commit sin, nor ever knew of sin, but through His most holy obedience, blood and death hath made satisfaction for all my sins and the sins of the whole world. Receive me, O Father, for the sake of this Saviour again into grace, and do not permit his bitter sufferings and death and his perfect precious ransom, which he has paid Thee for my sins to be lost by me, poor sinner, but that it may strengthen me. And I will then praise and bless Thee, here in time and there in eternity. Amen.

Prayer in great Weakness of Faith. O Lord, I know it now of a truth that all men have not faith. I believe, dear Lord, help my unbelief! Do not break the bruised reed, nor quench the smoking flax; O Jesus, Thou who sittest at the right hand of God, make intercession for me, that my faith may not cease. Be the author and finisher of my faith, wherewith I shall be able to quench all the fiery darts of the wicked one. Grant me that I believe, although I do not see, and thus be saved. Amen.

Prayer that God would hereafter keep us from sin, and if we sin, that He would not reckon it to our account. O thou kind and merciful God, Thou dear Father in heaven, Thou hast out of grace and divine love, bestowed upon us Thy dear Son, and with Him all grace, life and salvation. We pray Thee, dear Father, preserve unto us this blessed treasure and heavenly gift, the gracious countenance of Thy dear Son, Jesus Christ, that we may never lose Him through unthankfulness, or otherwise be deprived of Him. We are indeed poor, miserable and frail beings, who fall from one sin into another; we now sin in thought, now in word and deed, and it is with difficulty that we stand. Here we never find rest and peace; the devil watches our very thoughts, stirs them up, and fans the passions into flame, the world watches our words and deeds, walk and life, and gives us much offense and occasion to sin, our own flesh also never rests, besides yet all the occasional sins, vices and weaknesses which daily beset us, and which terribly trouble our conscience, entirely destroy the joy of our heart and turn it into sorrow and sadness. Therefore we pray Thee, Thou kind and merciful God, that when, as it may happen, we have become negligent and unthankful, and do not so walk as we should—O do Thou still remain our gracious God; be Thou friendly towards us, comfort us in goodness and mercy, do not hold us accountable or make us suffer for our manifold sins, but purge our hearts and consciences by Thy word, in order that we may serve Thee in sorrow and joy, magnify, honor and praise Thee in time and in eternity. Amen.

Prayer in view of the Sufferings of Christ. Alas! my Lord Jesus Christ, when I behold Thee, as Thou wast in the garden bowed down with heartfelt sorrow, and in great anguish didst sweat drops of blood, as Thou wast afterwards taken prisoner, bound, and during the whole night and hour of darkness mocked and insulted, in the morning early as the innocent Lamb accused, whipped with scourges, and finally sentenced to death, suspended on the cross, pierced in your hands and feet with ruthless nails, and not a member of Thy most holy body remaining without a wound:—Alas! when I see all this, I see nothing but my sins, guilt and iniquities which brought Thee into this plight, and for the sake of which Thou didst freely enter into such anguish and distress, into such sadness, pain and suffering. Alas! my Lord, it is all my guilt for which Thou didst suffer—I am the cause of it all. How wonderful are the ways and purposes of God! The Innocent One must pay for the guilt of the guilty, the Good One must suffer the punishments of the wicked. The Lord must atone the guilt of the servant, and that which sinful man has brought upon himself God must bear. O Thou Son of the living God, how great is Thy love and favor towards us mortals! What hast Thou not done and suffered to redeem me, a poor lost sinner, and to deliver me from death and eternal damnation. I have done evil, and Thou art punished; I have sinned, and Thou must atone. I have been disobedient, and Thou must for my disobedience be overwhelmed with such anguish and distress. Alas! Thou Lord of Glory, what can I give Thee in return for this Thy great goodness and faithfulness which Thou hast shown towards me! Wherewith shall I, poor needy mortal, requite such unspeakable benefit? Alas! my Lord, it shall forever remain unrequited. There is no service in heaven or on earth whereby to pay Thee sufficiently for it. It is Thy pure grace and favor towards me, a poor sinner, and that remains by me forever unrequited, forever unmerited. And since I have nothing wherewithall to pay my debt, therefore my heart shall evermore thank Thee for what Thou hast done to me, and I shall magnify, glorify and praise Thy name now and forever. Amen.

Prayer for true Conversion. Almighty God, merciful Father! Every day Thy voice calling me to repentance and grace resounds in my ears, encouraging me and all sinful souls unto conversion: Return, thou backsliding Israel, saith the Lord, and I will not cause mine anger to fall upon you; for I am merciful, saith the Lord, and I will not keep anger forever. Only acknowledge thine iniquity, that thou hast transgressed against the Lord, thy God. But alas! I am not sufficient of myself, as of myself to convert myself unto Thee. As little as the Ethiopian can change his skin and as little as the leopard can change its spots, so little can I cease to do evil and do good by my natural powers, inasmuch as the thoughts and intents of my heart are inclined to evil from my youth up continually. Has Thy grace wrought so much in me that I have determined that I will arise and reconcile myself with Thee on account of my sins, and offer unto Thee a broken and contrite heart, yet, alas! satan, the accursed one, will cast a thousandfold hindrances in the way. My own sinful flesh and blood prevent me, that the good that I will I cannot accomplish, but remain in sin and finally be destroyed therein. Wherefore, Abba, dear Father, I bend and bow my knees in deep humility before Thee, and ask for the sake of Thy infinite mercy: convert me, O Lord, and I shall be converted, help me, and I shall be helped, let Thy grace, my God, not be in vain in me, but as Thou hast given to will, so do Thou also give to accomplish it. Destroy the wantonness of the infernal villain, prevent the suggestions of my perverted heart, that my holy resolution may not be hindered or entirely destroyed. Open my eyes that I may heartily know, painfully lament, and bitterly bewail my sins. Give me a divine sorrow over my transgressions, which will bring repentance unto salvation, which may never be repented of. Do Thou not, O Lord, permit me to be destroyed under the burden of sin, nor to despair with Cain and Judas, but do Thou turn to me, and be merciful unto me, behold my misery and affliction, and forgive all my sins. Show me Thy dear and merciful heart, Father, which desireth not the death of a sinner, but that he may be converted and live; speak gently to my soul, and say that mercy shall go for justice, and that Thou wilt no more remember my transgressions. Show me with the finger of Thy divine grace unto Jesus, the crucified one, how he died for my sins and rose again for my justification. Open to me for a refuge his bloody wounds, in which so many poor sinners have found comfort and salvation. Create also a clean heart within me and renew a right spirit within me; cast me not away from Thy countenance and take not Thy Holy Spirit from me; comfort me again with Thy help, and the joyful Spirit preserve me in a firm resolution to amend my sinful life, and as long as I live to serve Thee in righteousness and holiness, as is pleasing in Thy sight. O Lord, hear me, alas! Lord! be merciful, O Lord! hearken to remember and do what I ask, for Jesus Christ's sake. Amen!

Prayers for Work and Protection

Prayer for a proper Performance of One's Duties. Merciful and faithful God! Thou hast commanded, that every man should pursue a certain calling and be faithful in the same. Thou seest and knowest, therefore, omniscient Lord, what my duties are, and that I can do nothing without Thy grace, power and blessing, but that I can err in various ways; therefore I sincerely pray Thee, to strengthen my reasoning faculties, to bestow upon me bold and undaunted courage, that I may act reasonably and overcome all rising difficulties, and thus accomplish through Thy paternal guidance a desirable and blessed object. O my God, I trust in Thee, let me not be ashamed, let not mine enemies triumph over me, yea, let none that wait on Thee be ashamed. Show me Thy ways, O Lord, teach me Thy paths; for Thou art the God of my salvation, on Thee do I wait all the day. Preserve my soul, deliver me and sustain me in my troubles. Let me not be ashamed, for I trust in Thee. O my God, be not far from me, make haste to help me, O Lord, my salvation! Amen. Amen. Amen.

Prayer before Labour. Eternal and Merciful God! I would now take up my work anew, and cheerfully lay hold upon the task of my proper calling, into which Thou hast placed me Thy servant, and thus Labour according to my talents received from Thee, that I might through them serve my neighbour and earn my daily bread. I would therefore pray Thee with all my heart, to bestow upon me knowledge, prudence, understanding and health for the performance of my Labour and work, according to Thy grace-abounding promise, and to further and bless the same, that not only its beginning be well done, but that I may also, through Thy paternal assistance and in Thy name, profitably finish it, and at all times perform the duties of my calling in Thy fear with a good conscience. Into Thy hands I commend my work; grant that my undertakings be successful, and that I may accomplish the work begun in Thy name, that the light may ever be shining upon my path, unto Thy honor and praise and the welfare of myself and friends and neighbours, through Thy dear Son Jesus Christ, our Lord, Amen. O Lord Jesus, in Thy name and upon Thy Word I will let down my net. O Lord, help, O Lord, let my work prosper. Amen.

Prayer for Divine Blessing upon the Work of One's Calling. Lord God! Thou hast assigned work to every man according to his abilities, and it is Thy will, that we should eat our daily bread in the sweat of our face, until we return again unto dust, and that we should live by the work of our hands and prosper; behold, upon Thy word I will begin anew the work of my calling, grant that my efforts and Labours be not in vain, but help that I may work with my hands the thing which is good, that I may have to give to him that needeth. Bestow upon me Thy favor and blessing at all times, for upon it depend all things, that I may accomplish my work and do wrong to no one, so that I may honor the Lord with my substance and provide for those near to me, especially for my own household. Bless us more and more, bless our substance and all that we have, for Thy blessing enriches us without the anxieties of the busy hand. Lord, gladden my heart and make cheerful my countenance, give me health, life and Thy blessing. All this, however, I ask of Thee in submission to Thy holy will, Lord, hear my prayer. Into Thy hands I commend my ways, in Thee I hope, Thou wilt do all things well. The Lord be praised daily. Amen.

Prayer before beginning any Important Work. Lord, Thou doest great things, which are unconceivable, and wonders innumerable, Thou whose strength is mighty in weakness; I call upon Thee, the Most High, to prosper the work of my hands and graciously help me to accomplish this work, which I have undertaken with entire confidence in Thee. Lord God, strengthen me in this hour, and depart not from Thy servant, whose hope is in Thee, and without Thee can do nothing. Prepare me with strength from on high, and give me the wisdom which is continually about Thy throne, that it may be with me and direct my Labours. All depends upon Thy divine blessing; wherefore remember me, O Lord, and bless all I do and all I leave undone, in order that I may begin and accomplish my work prudently and successfully. May my actions be pleasing unto Thee, assist me by Thy advice, in order that I may be able most profitably to begin, continue and finish my work. For unto Thee do I commit the beginning and the accomplishment of my Labours, and unto Thee will I thankfully ascribe all praise for prospering the work of my hands. Amen. In Jesus name, Amen, Amen!

Thanks returned after Labour. Almighty, eternal and gracious God! I praise and thank Thee for Thy most holy presence and assistance, which Thou hast shown unto me this day, for without Thee I certainly could have done nothing, hence Thou alone art worthy to receive the praise. I beseech Thee, to permit these Labours to be pleasing unto Thee, and to redound to the well-being of myself and neighbours, both bodily and spiritually, through Jesus Christ our Lord, who with Thee and the Holy Ghost, true God, lives and reigns to all eternity. Amen.

Prayer during a Journey. O Lord Jesus Christ, Thou ever-gracious Lord and Saviour! Thou who hast become a guest and stranger for us upon earth, I come unto Thee humbled in heart, and beseech Thee, that Thou wouldst permit my whole life and walk to be acceptable unto Thee. Preserve me also upon this my journey by the protection of Thy beloved angels upon all my ways graciously from all evil and accident, misfortune and danger of soul and body, so that I may successfully accomplish my work and return again to my beloved ones, in health and in vigor. Unto Thee alone, O Lord, do I commit my body and soul, all that I have and possess, during my journey. Do Thou direct my course and way to my welfare and blessedness. In the mean time do Thou faithfully protect my loved ones at home, that we may meet each other again in health and happiness. And when I have finally accomplished my journey of life here in this world, receive me unto Thyself, into Thy glory, by a peaceful and a blessed death. Amen.

Thanksgiving after a safe Journey. Gracious God, heavenly Father, I thank Thee with my whole heart, that Thou hast in safety brought me to my journey's end, and that to my joy, Thy holy angels have led me back to my family. As a Father Thou hast also kept me from all evil, prevented robbers and murderers from killing me, wild beasts from tearing me to pieces, floods of water and other perils from destroying or injuring me. Thou hast led me in safety as the angel Raphael led the young Tobias. All this I owe to Thy paternal care and almighty protection. In mercy keep me and mine, take us under Thy mighty protection, and by Thy power preserve body and soul unto eternal life for Jesus Christ's sake. Amen.

Prayer in great Trouble and Danger. O almighty God and Father, who art ever ready to help, Thou seest the great trouble and danger in which we are living; we know of no counsel or help, and have no strength of ourselves to come out of trouble, therefore our eyes look unto Thee, who alone art our consolation, refuge and helper, and hast said: Call upon me in the day of trouble, I will deliver thee, and thou shalt glorify me. Our heart clings to Thy word of promise and in childlike humility and confidence seeks Thy face. O Lord, hide not Thy face, full of compassion, from us, and put not Thy children away in anger. Leave us not, neither forsake us, O God of our salvation, who workest salvation in the midst of the earth. Let Thy help also come unto us and be merciful unto us. O Lord, our God, in Thee do we put our trust and under the shadow of Thy wings do we make our refuge until these calamities be overpast. Turn again unto us and satisfy us early with Thy mercy and we will freely sacrifice unto Thee, we will praise Thy name, O Lord, for it is good. Make us glad according to the days wherein Thou hast afflicted us, and the years wherein we have seen evil. Give us help from trouble and we will praise Thee, and rejoice in Thy salvation all the days of our life. Amen.

Thanksgiving for Deliverance out of Tribulation. I will praise Thee, O Lord my God, with all my heart, and I will glorify Thy name forevermore. I will praise Thee for ever, because Thou canst do all things well. Behold, instead of peace I had great bitterness, but Thou hast in love to my soul delivered it from the pit of corruption. In my distress I called unto Thee, and Thou hast heard my voice, and my cry did enter into Thy ears, and Thou hast comforted me. Thou hast faithfully helped me, in mercy upheld my soul, and finally delivered me out of my great tribulation. My Lord and my God, what shall I render unto Thee for all the benefits which Thou daily bestowest? I will praise Thy name all the days of my life, I will magnify Thee among all Thy people, and Thy glory shall continually be in my mouth. Thy Spirit, O faithful God, enable me to pay my vows and never to forget the benefits Thou hast bestowed upon my soul. Let me spread Thy praise in time, and also in Eternity, together with the elect, sing everlasting Hallelujahs to the honor of Thy name. Amen.

Morning Prayer of a sick Person. O Thou faithful God and Father of our Lord Jesus Christ! I will thank and praise Thee that Thou hast so mercifully kept, protected and strengthened me in my weakness. In Jesus' name, turn unto me to-day and the remaining days of my life, cleanse me from my sin, comfort me by Thy grace, strengthen me by Thy power, lead me by Thy Holy Spirit, that I may live and suffer in accordance with Thy will. I commit my sick body and my soul into Thy holy hands, let Thy holy angel have charge concerning me that the wicked one may have no power or influence over me, through Jesus Christ, our only comfort and Redeemer, in the power of the Holy Ghost. Amen.

Evening Prayer of a sick Person. Thanks be unto Thee, my God and Father, that Thou hast this day so mercifully succored me. Thy grace, Thy power, Thy comfort and Thy Spirit be with me in my sickness and help me through this night also. I commit my body and soul into Thy hands, Thy holy angels have charge concerning me, that the wicked one may have no power over me, through Jesus Christ, Thy dear Son, our Lord. Amen.

Prayer of a penitent in Sickness. Almighty God and Father, because of sin Thou appointest over men all manner of diseases, but in particular bodily sickness, that they may not perish with the world. I come unto Thee with my load of sins and confess that on account of these I have deserved not only this sickness, but also eternal damnation, being a child of wrath by nature and sold under sin, besides having, all the days of my life, transgressed all Thy commandments a countless number of times. I take my refuge in Thy boundless mercy. Enter not into judgment with me, for in Thy sight shall no man living be justified. Remember not the sins of my youth, nor my transgressions, but for Thy name's sake pardon mine iniquity, for it is great. Remove Thy stroke away from me and hearken unto the voice of my cry, hold not Thy peace at my tears. Spare me that I may recover strength, before I go hence, and be no more. Affectionate Father, behold, for peace I have great bitterness, in love deliver my soul from the pit of corruption and cast all my sins behind Thy back. Consider also my bodily affliction and take it away or alleviate it by Thy comfort. Give me patience, help me to bear my cross, or save me under it. Thy will be done. Do with me, O God, as it seemeth good unto Thee. I am Thine, in Thee I would remain. Amen.

Thanksgiving after Recovery. I thank Thee, Lord, almighty God, that Thou hast so paternally visited and chastised me on account of my sins. Yea, Lord, I am glad that Thou hast humiliated me, that I might learn Thy ways. O my God, how often have I, like Hezekiah, thought: Mine age is departed, and is removed from me as a shepherd's tent; I have cut off like a weaver my life; he will cut me off with pining sickness; from day even to night wilt Thou make an end of me. But, my God, I see that my sickness was not unto death, but unto the glory of God, that Thou, my Lord Jesus Christ, mightest thereby be glorified. For Thou hast had mercy upon me, and hast cast all my sins behind Thee, and hast prolonged my life. I heartily thank Thee, my God, that Thou hast revived and strengthened me, that I can behold Thy holy temple, and attend to my duties. Thy goodness it is, Lord, else I should long since have perished. O, how often will I think of Thy chastening rod, and will fear Thee all my life and guard against Thy wrath. Help now, O Lord my God, that with renewed health I may also begin a new life. Grant, that I may always glorify Thy name, and Thy praise be continually found in my mouth. Guide me by Thy Holy Spirit, that I may live to Thy honor, and not yield my members as instruments of unrighteousness to serve sin, but as instruments of righteousness to serve Thee my God, that I may sing Thy hymns, and praise and glorify Thee in Thy church. Amen.

Church Prayers

Before going to Church. Merciful God and Father! Thou seest, that by reason of my depraved nature I have no delight in Thy word, and that I so easily permit the devil, my own flesh and blood, the children of the world, also false teachers and preachers and other trivial causes keep me away from it, and that I am too indolent and careless to hear and preserve Thy word. Therefore I now pray Thee, O eternal God, forgive me this my inbred indolence, and do Thou give me a heart willing and apt to hear and meditate upon Thy word. Awake in me such an earnest longing that I may have a desire after the sincere milk of the divine word, as new-born babes. Help me, that I may find my chief delight in Thy word. May there be nothing in this world dearer to me than Thy word; may I love it more than gold and all fine gold, and always regard it as my best treasure. And as I, alas! have lived to see the time which Thy dear Son Himself foretold, that false Christs should arise and do wonders, so that, if it were possible, even the elect should be deceived, I pray Thee that Thou wouldst graciously defend and protect me from error and false doctrine. Keep me in Thy truth, for Thy word is truth, that I may cling to the same as heavenly truth, and remain steadfast in the same unto death. Grant this for the sake of the honor of Thy most holy and blessed name. Amen.

Morning Prayer of a Communicant. Lord Jesus, I this morning rejoice that I, with other pious Christians, am permitted to receive Thy body and blood in, with and under the consecrated bread and wine. O! how my soul longs for the courts of the Lord and for the holy altar. As the hart panteth after the water brooks, so panteth my soul after Thee, O my God. For Thou art my Shepherd, I shall not want. O, Lord Jesus, as Thou hast begun the good work in me a poor miserable man, so also accomplish the same in mercy, through the gracious power of the Holy Spirit unto Thy name's glory and unto my own welfare and eternal salvation. Dear Redeemer, I am, it is true, not worthy that I should come under Thy roof, but Thy grace, which is all-sufficient, make me worthy and amply qualify me, that the precious food and drink of Thy true body and blood may quicken my soul in this heavenly feast of joy and love. Clothe me with the garment of salvation and with the robe of Thy righteousness by a true faith, that I may not be found among the pretending guests and would-be-Christians, but may be a worthy partaker at Thy table and receive all Thy gracious treasures which Thou hast acquired for me. O Lord Jesus, may Thy grace be and remain with me, as I ever put my trust in Thee. May Thy visitation preserve my spirit, my life and walk. And whatever else is needful, grant Thou, O Lord, unto me in this life and in the life hereafter. Give me true repentance, renew my heart, deliver my body and soul. O Lord! hear this my desire, and do not permit my prayer to remain unanswered, that I may be acceptable unto Thee in time and in eternity. Amen, in Jesus' name, Amen.

Prayer for a worthy Partaking of the Holy Supper. Behold me, Dear Saviour, As I Come Relying on Thy Gracious Invitation. May I find favor in Thine eyes, Thou Lover of Life. For who am I that Thou shouldst so friendly call me? Were I even holier than the angels, yet would I not be worthy of this repast; how then should I be worthy, seeing that I am of impure lips, yea, an abomination and offensive, if Thou doest not make me worthy? Therefore come Thou to my succor with Thy grace, and prepare me. Thou hast said: Whosoever cometh to me, Thou wilt in no wise cast out. Then take my soul into Thy favor, according to Thy great mercies. Dear Jesus, remember that of myself I have indeed much evil, but nothing good; so help me for Thy great goodness' sake. O see how poor and miserable I am! Remember Thy faithfulness, O Saviour of the world, and fill my heart with grace. O! how I long to appear at Thy table with glowing devotion and becoming reverence in full faith, but where is the power to do, if I do not receive it of Thee, thou Author and Finisher of my faith? Therefore give Thou unto me whatsoever is pleasing to Thee. Graciously take from me whatsoever displeases Thee, or cover it, at least, I most humbly pray Thee, with the cloak of Thy righteousness. O! blessed is the soul that finds favor with Thee! Open Thou mine eyes that I may behold the wonders in Thy ordinances. Rouse my heart, and free me of all strange thoughts, increase my hope, inflame my desire, make ardent my devotion, purge me of all uncleanness, and sanctify me wholly, that I may approach with joyful confidence, that I may receive with pure mouth and holy heart, and with heartfelt desire eat and drink unto the life, welfare and blessing of my soul. Amen.

Thanksgiving after Partaking of the Holy Supper. Lord Jesus Christ, I give Thee most hearty thanks and praise, that Thou hast again washed me, a poor sinful being, of all my transgressions, and, for the most certain assurance of such washing and forgiveness of all my sins, hast permitted me to eat of Thy true body, and to drink of Thy true blood, and, taking me as an impure child after such cleansing, hast again received me into the fatherly arms of Thy grace and mercy, and doest thus show and present me blameless, pure and without fault unto Thy heavenly Father.

I pray Thee most heartily and from my whole soul, that, after Thy great benefit, Thou wouldst yet add this in abundance, and graciously grant me Thy grace through the working of the Holy Ghost, that I may be truly sensible of Thy great goodness, thankfully receive it, and from my heart magnify and praise Thee during my whole life. And do Thou further work in me through Thy Holy Ghost, and effect that I]also may heartily forgive my neighbour anything he may have done against me, as Thou, O Lord, hast pardoned and forgiven all my great and numerous transgressions, yea, and hast entirely wiped them out of Thy remembrance; that I may also love my neighbour, and from my heart show him all manner of good, even as Thou, O Lord, hast shown unto me more than I am able to thank for; in order that Thou, O good and faithful God, in us mayest be magnified and praised together with the Father and Holy Ghost throughout all ages. Amen.

Grace

(Prayers before Meat)

The eyes of all wait upon Thee, O Lord: Thou givest them their meat in due season, Thou openest Thy liberal hand, and satisfiest the desire of every living thing. Amen.

Come, Lord Jesus, be Thou our guest,
And let all Thou giv'st us be blest. Amen.

We thank Thee, dear Son, that Thou hast again opened Thy bountiful hand to supply our wants; grant that we may receive this food with thanksgiving and gratitude and in Thy fear, and grant, O Lord! that whatsoever we do, whether we eat or drink, all may be done to Thy name's honor and glory, through Jesus Christ, our Saviour. Amen.

O Lord God, heavenly Father, bless unto us these Thy gifts, which of Thy tender kindness Thou hast bestowed upon us, through Jesus Christ, our Lord. Amen.

German Reformed Church Daily Devotional

On Waking from Sleep.

O God, thou art my God; early will I seek thee. Ps. 63. 1.

I laid me down and slept; I awaked; for the Lord sustained me. Ps. 3. 5.

I will lift up mine eyes unto the hills, from whence cometh my help. My help cometh from the Lord, which made heaven and earth. Ps.100 1, 2.

My voice shalt thou hear in the morning, O Lord; in the morning will I direct my prayer unto thee, and will look up. Ps. 5. 3.

Almighty and most merciful God, who didst in the beginning create the light, and who dost cause the sun to rise every morning; dispel from my soul the clouds of darkness by the light of Thy truth, that in Thy light I may see light, and that rising with Christ, who is the Resurrection and the Life, I may walk in newness of life, to the praise of Thy glorious name.

Unto Thee, O Lord, my Maker and Redeemer, I humbly offer up myself, my body and soul, my health and strength, all that I am, and all that I have, as a living sacrifice and thanksgiving.

Heavenly Father, blessed be Thy holy name for Thy merciful protection during the past night. Grant that I may spend this day, and all the days of my life, in Thy holy service, and grow daily in grace, and in the knowledge of our Lord and Saviour Jesus Christ.

Whilst Washing and Dressing.

Wash me thoroughly from mine iniquity, and cleanse me from my sin. Ps. 51. 2.

Ye are washed, ye are sanctified, ye are justified in the name of the Lord Jesus, and by the Spirit of our God. 1 Cor. 6. 11

The blood of Jesus Christ cleanseth us from all sin. 1 John 1. 7.

Wash me, O Lord Jesus, lover of my soul, with Thine own precious blood, which cleanseth from all sin. Clothe me with the robe of Thy righteousness, and adorn me with the graces of Thy Spirit, that I may glorify Thee in my daily walk and conversation, and enjoy Thee forever.

When entering on the duties of the day.

I must work the works of him that sent me while it is day: the night cometh, when no man can work. John 9. 4.

Whatsoever thy hand findeth to do, do it with thy might; for there is no work, nor device, nor knowledge, nor wisdom in the grave, whither thou goest. Eccles. 9. 10.

Watch and pray that ye enter not into temptation; the spirit indeed is willing, but the flesh is weak. Matt. 26. 41.

O Lord God Almighty, who has safely brought me to the beginning of this day, defend me by Thy power; guard me against sin and error; and so order the events of my life, and so sanctify my thoughts and deeds, that they may promote Thy glory, and the welfare of my fellowmen, through Jesus Christ our Saviour.

Enable me, O Lord, by Thy heavenly grace to discharge the duties of this day with supreme regard to Thy glory; to withstand its temptations with Christian courage; to submit to its trials with humble resignation; knowing that all things are from eternity foreseen and ordained by Thine infinite wisdom and mercy, and must work together for good to those that love Thee.

Direct me, O Lord, in all my doings, with Thy most gracious favor, and further me with Thy continual help; that in all my works, begun, continued, and ended in Thee, I may glorify Thy holy name, and finally, by Thy mercy, attain everlasting life: through Jesus Christ our Lord.

Before and after meals.

Every good and perfect gift is from above, and cometh down from the Father of lights, with whom is no variableness, neither shadow of turning. James 1. 17.

Sanctify, O Lord, this food of Thy mercy to our use, and ourselves to Thy service, through Jesus Christ our Saviour. Amen.

Give us this day our daily bread; forgive us our sins; and save us in Thy kingdom, through Jesus Christ our Saviour. Amen.

We thank Thee, O God, from whom cometh down every good and perfect gift, for these new provisions of Thy bounty. Feed our immortal souls with the bread of life, and admit us at last to the table of Thy saints in heaven, through Jesus Christ our Lord. Amen.

On retiring to rest.

Behold, he that keepeth Israel, shall neither slumber nor sleep. The Lord is they keeper; the Lord is thy shade upon thy right hand. Ps. 121i. 4, 5.

He shall give his angels charge over thee, to keep thee in all thy ways. Ps. 96. 11.

He that dwelleth in the secret places of the Most High, shall abide under the shadow of the Almighty. I will say of the Lord, He is my refuge, my fortress, my God; in him will I trust. Ps. 91. 1, 2.

Though I walk through the valley of the shadow of death, I will fear no evil; for thou art with me; thy rod and thy staff they comfort me. Ps. 23. 4.

I will lay me down in peace and take my rest in Thy name, O Lord, who makest me to dwell in safety. Keep me from sin and harm; refresh me with wholesome sleep, raise me up again to the praise of Thy name, and bring me at last to life eternal. Amen.

Into Thy hands, O Lord and Keeper of Israel, I commend my body, soul, and spirit. Defend me from the terrors of the night, and preserve me from all evil. Keep me mindful of the vanity of life, the certainty of death, and the judgment to come, and prepare me for a happy end, through Jesus Christ our Savior. Amen.

Most Merciful Father, who hast safely brought me to the end of this day, take me under the wings of Thy protection for the coming night. Defend my body from harm, and my soul from sin. Keep me mindful of my end; and when heart and flesh fail, be Thou the strength of my heart, and my portion for ever. Amen.

At Midnight.

The day of the Lord will come as a thief in the night.—2 Pet. iii. 10.

Be ye also ready; for the Son of man cometh at an hour when ye think not.—Luke xii. 40.

O Jesus Christ, who hast compared Thy second coming to that of the bridegroom at midnight, let this cry, "Behold the bridegroom cometh," continually sound in my ear, and grant that I may always have oil in my lamp, and be in readiness to meet Thee. Amen.

Grant, O God, that I may live in Thy fear, die in Thy peace, rest in my grave under Thy protection, rise by Thy power to the resurrection of the just, and be numbered with Thy saints in glory everlasting, through Jesus Christ our Lord; to whom with Thee and the Holy Ghost be all honor and praise, for ever and ever. Amen.

Scottish Metrical Psalms

Taken from the Scottish Psalter of 1650

Psalm 8

How excellent in all the earth
Lord, our Lord, is thy name!
Who hast thy glory far advanced
above the starry frame.

From infants' and from sucklings' mouth
thou didest strength ordain,
For thy foes' cause, that so thou
might'st th' avenging foe restrain.

When I look up unto the heav'ns
which thine own fingers framed,
Unto the moon, and to the stars
which were by thee ordained;

Then say I, What is man
that he remembered is by thee?
Or what the son of man, that thou
so kind to him should'st be?

For thou a little lower hast
him than the angels made;
With glory and with dignity
thou crowned hast his head.

Of thy hands' works thou mad'st him lord
all under's feet didst lay;
All sheep and oxen, yea, and beasts
that in the field do stray;

Fowls of the air, fish of the sea
all that pass through the same.
How excellent in all the earth :
Lord, our Lord, is thy name!

Psalm 24

The earth belongs unto the Lord, and all that it contains;
The world that is inhabited, and all that there remains.
For the foundations thereof he on the seas did lay,
And he hath it established upon the floods to stay.

Who is the man that shall ascend into the hill of God?
Or who within his holy place shall have a firm abode?

Whose hands are clean, whose heart is pure, and unto vanity
Who hath not lifted up his soul, nor sworn deceitfully.

He from th' Eternal shall receive the blessing him upon,
And righteousness, ev'n from the God of his salvation.
This is the generation that after him enquire,
O Jacob, who do seek thy face with their whole heart's desire.

Ye gates, lift up your heads on high; ye doors that last for aye,
 Be lifted up, that so the King : of glory enter may.
But who of glory is the King? The mighty Lord is this;
Ev'n that same Lord, that great in might : and strong in battle is.

Ye gates, lift up your heads; ye doors, doors that do last for aye,
Be lifted up, that so the King : of glory enter may.
But who is he that is the King of glory? who is this?
The Lord of hosts, and none but he, the King of glory is.

Psalm 46

God is our refuge and our strength,
in straits a present aid;
Therefore, although the earth remove,
we will not be afraid:
Though hills amidst the seas be cast;
Though waters roaring make,
And troubled be; yea, though the hills,
By swelling seas do shake.

A river is, whose streams do glad
The city of our God;
The holy place, wherein the Lord
Most high hath his abode.
God in the midst of her doth dwell;
nothing shall her remove:
The Lord to her an helper will,
and that right early, prove.

The heathen raged tumultuously,
the kingdoms moved were:
The Lord God uttered his voice,
the earth did melt for fear.
The Lord of hosts upon our side
doth constantly remain:
The God of Jacob's our refuge,
us safely to maintain.

Come, and behold what wondrous works
have by the Lord been wrought;
Come, see what desolations he
Upon the earth hath brought.

Unto the ends of all the earth
wars into peace he turns:
The bow he breaks, the spear he cuts,
in fire the chariot burns.

Be still, and know that I am God;
among the heathen I
Will be exalted; I on earth
will be exalted high.
The Lord of hosts is on our side
Our safety to maintain
The God of Jacob doth for us
A refuge high remain.

Psalm 53

That there is not a God, the fool
doth in his heart conclude:
They are corrupt, their works are vile,
not one of them doth good.
The Lord upon the sons of men
from heav'n did cast his eyes,
To see if any one there was
that sought God and was wise.

They altogether filthy are,
they all are backward gone;
And there is none that doeth good,
no, not so much as one.
These workers of iniquity,
do they not know at all,
That they my people eat as bread,
and on God do not call?

Ev'n there they were afraid, and stood
with trembling, all dismayed,
Whereas there was no cause at all
why they should be afraid:
For God his bones that thee besieged
hath scattered all abroad;
Thou hast confounded them, for they
despised are of God.

Let Isr'el's help from Zion come
when back the Lord shall bring
His captives, Jacob shall rejoice,
and Israel shall sing.

Psalm 146

Praise God. The Lord praise, O my soul.
I'll praise God while I live;
While I have being to my God
in songs I'll praises give.
Trust not in princes, nor man's son,
in whom there is no stay:
His breath departs, to's earth he turns;
that day his thoughts decay.

O happy is that man and blest,
whom Jacob's God doth aid;
Whose hope upon the Lord doth rest,
and on his God is stayed:
Who made the earth and heavens high,
who made the swelling deep,
And all that is within the same;
who truth doth ever keep:

Who righteous judgment executes
for those oppressed that be,
Who to the hungry giveth food;
God sets the pris'ners free.
The Lord doth give the blind their sight,
the bowed down doth raise:
The Lord doth dearly love all those
that walk in upright ways.

The stranger's shield, the widow's stay,
the orphan's help, is he:
But yet by him the wicked's way
turned upside down shall be.
The Lord shall reign for evermore
thy God, O Zion, he
Reigns to all generations.
Praise to the Lord give ye.

Acknowledgments

All of the material in this little book was digitised by other people and made available freely through the net, and is why this is being sold only at the cost of printing.

The Calvin prayers are taken from the website of St Matthew's Church, Westminster (https://www.stmw.org/), as was the third Luther prayer; the morning and evening prayers of Calvin come from the website of the Gospel Coalition (https://www.thegospelcoalition.org/) and the other Luther prayers from the blog of 'Internet Monk' Chaplain Michael Spencer (https://internetmonk.com/). The Bucer prayers come from the blog of Prof. R. Scott Clark (https://rscottclark.org/).

The Book Of Common Prayer material came from the Gutenberg edition, [EBook #29622], produced by Elaine Laizure
http://www.gutenberg.org/cache/epub/29622/pg29622.html

Compline and some psalms came from Justus.Anglican.Org.

Other prayers, and the Reformation-era illustrations, come from internet searches.

The German sources are:
- Johann Habermann's *Morning and Evening Prayers for All Days of the Week* etc., also published as *The Christian's Companion:* Translator: Emil H. Rausch, Release Date: January 17, 2011 [EBook #34994] Produced by Stephen Hutcheson
  http://www.gutenberg.org/files/34994/34994-h/34994-h.htm
- *Little Treasure of Prayers*: Translation Of The German larger "Treasure of Prayers" [Gebets-Schatz] of the Evangelical Lutheran Church, Columbus, Ohio: the Lutheran Book Concern. J. L. Trauger, agent, 1888. Produced by Stephen Hutcheson, David Edwards, Peter Vachuska
  http://www.gutenberg.org/files/35737/35737-h/35737-h.htm
- *A Liturgy or Order of Christian Worship* of the German Reformed Church, transcribed by Prof. E.J. Hutchinson at the Calvinist International wenbsite
  https://calvinistinternational.com/

The Scottish Metrical Psalms came from the website Music for the Church of God (http://www.cgmusic.org/).

This publication is for personal devotional use and is not made, nor should it be distributed, not financial profit.

Printed in Great Britain
by Amazon